HOW THEY MADE THEIR MILLIONS

TURING DREAMS INTO MILLIONS

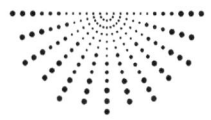

VIJAY PEDURU

VOL-1

Copyright © Vijay Peduru

ALL RIGHTS RESERVED

No part of this publication may be reproduced, stored in or introduced into a retrieval system, or transmitted, in any form or by any means (electronically, mechanical, photocopying, recording or otherwise), without the prior written permission of both the copyright owner and the publisher of this book.

Re-selling through electronic outlets (like Amazon, Barnes and Nobles or E-bay) without permission of the publisher is illegal and punishable by law.

The scanning, uploading, and distribution of this book via the Internet or via any other means without the permission of the publisher is illegal and punishable by law.

Please purchase only authorized editions and no not participate in or encourage electronic piracy of copyrightable materials.

Your support of the author's right is appreciated.

ISBN-13:978-0-578-40533-9 | ISBN-10:0-578-40533-4

Cover Design: Vijay Peduru

To

The ever-awesome Sadhguru
Yogi, mystic and founder of Isha Foundation

I believed that Business was about
extracting more from others than what I gave.
I was in deep distress and lost my passion.

Sadhguru showed me a radical approach to Business
To give away more than what I received.
I acted and behold, business was joy,
Passion and profits flowed.

CONTENTS

Will this book make you Successful?	vii
Short wisdom	xi
1. Instagram	1
2. Pandora	21
3. Ben & Jerry's Ice Cream	33
4. Cheese Cake Factory	51
5. Huffington Post	65
6. Wrigley's Gum	91
7. Minecraft	109
8. CPK- California Pizza Kitchen	127
9. Craigslist	137
10. Hershey's Chocolates	155
11. LifeisGood	169
12. WhatsApp	183
Closing wisdom	203
Bonus Material	205
About the Author	207

WILL THIS BOOK MAKE YOU SUCCESSFUL?

Can you be a Rich and successful Entrepreneur?

There are 2 paths

First
way is to figure things out all by yourself

If you figure things out all by yourself

There are 3 disadvantages.

| Live in stress and constant fear of failure | Chances are high that you may not succeed. | You could waste 10-20 years and still remain a failure |

Please proceed to next page

The second way is to do what every successful Entrepreneur does.

Learn from other successful entrepreneurs.

| Steve Jobs(Apple) learnt from Edward Land, Poloroid founder | Warren Buffet learnt from Benjamin Graham | Jeff Bezos(Amazon) learnt from Sam Walton, Walmart founder |

There are 3 Advantages

| Be Successful and Rich in a very short time without many bruises and failures | Live with Confidence because you are learning from the best and Super-Successful | Live an awesome life, the way you want it, filled with passion and Joy. |

Please proceed to next page

You choose the path you wish to take.

if you choose the first path loaded with a high chance of business failure, You may probably not like this book.

if you choose the second path, welcome to the elite few who are committed to turn their dreams into multi-million-dollar successful ventures.

This book you are holding will show you the second path

Each millionaire founder story in this book, has million-dollar-worth hidden lessons if you can notice and grab them.

As many successful entrepreneurs like Steve jobs, Warren Buffet and Jeff Bezos showed, your chances of becoming rich and successful are way high, if you learn from other successful entrepreneurs.

Your mission if you choose to accept it, is to Choose to learn from Successful entrepreneurs and live a rich and happy life.

SHORT WISDOM

"We're here to put a dent in the universe."

~Steve Jobs, Founder of Apple

1
INSTAGRAM

STARTING IN A ONE-BEDROOM APARTMENT TO SELLING IT FOR $1 BILLION IN 2 YEARS

Kevin Systrom left a well-paying job and started a Foursquare clone, but it did not work and so he started listening to his users.

His users wanted photo sharing and he scraped his old idea even though he put in a lot of effort and focused on building an app to share photos.

Kevin then accidentally stumbled into this idea for Instagram, a social network using photos thanks to his girlfriend, a stray dog, and a beach.

It took off like a weed and Facebook came calling and bought Instagram for $1 billion.

Kevin Systrom was born to Diane and Douglas Systrom on 30th December 1983, in Holliston, Massachusetts.

Kevin's mother worked at Monster.com during the first tech startup boom and later at Zipcar.

She was always eager to learn new things and she learned to

snowboard at the age of 45. Kevin says she's the coolest mom with a tremendous energy. Kevin has a younger sister Kate.

As a kid, when Kevin was in fourth grade, he wanted to start companies in his classroom. He was charging people for candy out of his locker. Kevin says "I won't say I was a natural entrepreneur, I think I was actually pretty bad at that." People didn't really buy the candy, and people were like, "Why are you doing this?"

He used to push everyone, even kids he didn't know, to buy the candy. They thought he was a creepy guy.

During his teens, he learned to write code and he created programs that would prank his friends by appearing to hack their AOL Instant Messenger accounts. He wrote programs that allowed him to control their cursors or knock them offline.

His antics got the family AOL account blocked.

But when he moved to high school, his interest changed from computers to music. He wanted to be a DJ.

"I was obsessed with deejaying," he says.

There was a store nearby called Boston Beat an old-school, vinyl-record store on posh Newbury Street and he would email them every other day to get a job as a DJ.

He pestered them repeatedly and finally they let him in, and he worked a couple of hours a week as a music DJ.

Kevin was soon doing real DJ'ing at several other Boston club shows. Since he was still under 18, he got help from older friends to sneak into the clubs.

He used to stockpile giant stacks of records in a corner of his bedroom. If he liked something, he used to get very obsessed with it.

When it came time to apply to college, the obvious choice was Stanford, with its tech offerings and deep ties to Silicon Valley.

He got into Stanford with a planned focus on computer science, but once he got there, he found that the classes were more academic and not practical and not interesting.

So he switched to Stanford's management science and engineering program, which had a focus on more practical subjects like finance and economics.

Kevin spent his free time building websites, such as a Stanford version of Craigslist. Another site, which he called Photobox, was a place for his fraternity, Sigma Nu, to post and share photos from the latest keg party. Soon enough, he realized just how much photography interested him.

Slowly his interest in photography kept growing.

During a junior year abroad in Florence, he took a very high-end camera, but the Italian professor took that camera away and gave him a Holga, a cheap camera, first popular in China, that developed a cult following because of its low-fi, retro-style photos. Surprisingly, Kevin loved these photos. Plus they were using different chemicals to get a retro-look. He adored the aesthetic of the images. They looked hip.

During the summer before his senior year in college, Kevin interned at Odeo, a podcasting startup created by Evan Williams, who would go on to co-found Twitter.

One of the people working at Odeo full- time, while Kevin was interning there was Jack Dorsey, another Twitter co-founder, with Williams and Biz Stone. Kevin and Jack Dorsey hit it off, tweaking apps together for Odeo; Jack later helped Kevin to get key connections in the tech world.

"I learned so much from Ev and Jack, the whole thing was really eye-opening for me," says Kevin.

In his senior year at Stanford, Kevin got a lot of job opportunities to work at a number of tech companies, including Microsoft, but he took a marketing job at Google, which in many ways was the place to be for Stanford grads, eager to make their mark. He was paid about $60,000.

But Kevin wasn't writing code or working on cool new products, he was handling marketing projects for Gmail and Calendar. After two years, he managed to switch to Google's M&A

division, where he learned about big tech deals and the money it takes to do them.

Still, three years into his time at Google, Kevin grew restless. He had gone there straight out of college, and the large, corporate environment took its toll on someone who had always wanted to be an entrepreneur. "I always had this itch," he says. "I wanted to get back in the social space."

He left Google for a job at a social travel guide site called NextStop, which offered travel recommendations. NextStop was started by ex-googlers.

There he was able to do, more of what he had wanted all along: write code and create app-style programs for the site, including games revolving around photos.

"All of a sudden I had a new skill that I could actually put to use," says Kevin. "When you have an idea you could actually create it."

While at NextStop, he started noticing the rising tide of mobile, location-based gaming and social networking trends.

It was becoming more and more obvious to Kevin that he had to pursue his passion for photography and social sharing full-time. He was ready to start his own thing, something that married those two interests.

On nights and weekends, Kevin, who had no formal computer-coding training, poured his time and energy into side projects that, he says, would help him learn to code.

Kevin had developed a few business ideas in his spare time, but in late 2009, he decided to concentrate his attention on one business idea.

He says "classes/majors can prepare you to learn for the job, but doing the work is where you learn what you'll use every day."

Soon he found something he wanted to create: a site that would combine his passion for photos with location check-ins and social gaming, mimicking the then-surging Foursquare and Zynga, respectively.

He began working on his idea in his spare time and called the idea Burbn. He created a new word Burbn by removing letters from the word bourbon, which was his favorite whiskey.

He made a prototype of the app, which allowed for location-based photo sharing. In a sense, It was a mashup of Foursquare and Zynga.

"I figured I could build a prototype of the idea in HTML5 and get it to some friends," Kevin says

"Those friends ended up using the prototype without any branding elements or design at all."

The app's primary function was to let users check-in to locations, make future plans with acquaintances, earn points for hanging out with friends, and post pictures.

But there was just one thing missing and it was money. Kevin was still working full-time at Nextstop.com, so he would need an infusion of cash that would allow him to focus full time on developing his product.

For Kevin, his good fortune came over cocktails at the Madrone Art Bar in early 2010 at a party for Hunch, a start-up based in Silicon Valley.

At this party, Kevin met and showed the prototype to Steve Anderson, a Bay Area venture capitalist and founder of Baseline Ventures.

Though Burbn was still just an idea, Anderson committed $250,000. In the same round, Marc Andreessen and Ben Horowitz, one of Silicon Valley's top VC firms also invested $250,000 for a total of $500k.

Kevin was not sure if he should quit his job, because it was a great job with good team members. But he gathered up his courage and quit his job at NextStop. Incidentally, NextStop was bought by Facebook that July of the same year.

He launched Burbn in the living room of his one-bedroom San Francisco apartment and would often work on the prototype at a Coffee Bar in the Mission so that he could see other humans.

There he would sometimes bump into Mike Krieger, a Brazilian native who had graduated from Stanford's Mayfield program two years behind Kevin and was working on apps of his own.

Mike was working at a chat site called Meebo.

They had previously met at Stanford's Mayfield Fellows program, a nine-month work-study program at Stanford University, designed to educate eager young students in running technology companies.

On one occasion Kevin let Mike download his new check-in app. "I wasn't super enthusiastic about location-based things, but Burbn was the first one that I loved," Mike says noting it was the ability to view photos of his friends' various adventures that had him hooked.

A month later Kevin invited Mike to breakfast to convince him to quit Meebo and join Burbn as a cofounder. Mike's response was "Count me interested; we'll talk more."

Instead of quitting his job right away, Mike decided to work together first and see if it will work out. So, the pair field-tested the partnership, working on small programs after work and over weekends. After a few weeks, Mike was convinced that he could work well with Kevin.

So Mike quit Meebo and started what would be a three-month process to obtain a U.S. work visa.

In March 2010, Kevin's first hire and eventual co-founder Mike Krieger joined him.

Once Mike joined, they took a step back and looked at the product as it stood.

"We decided that if we were going to build a company, we wanted to focus on being really good at one thing."

Burbn was really too similar to Foursquare, he reasoned, which was becoming very popular. Burbn got a lot of hype in tech blogs, but it didn't really go anywhere.

It was "cluttered" and "overrun with features," but users were liking one piece of it and it was photo sharing and it was the most popular feature on their app.

So in August, the founders made an incredibly risky, but perhaps prophetic, decision: They'd scrap Burbn almost entirely in order to build an entirely new app from the ground up.

They had to build something new and decided to streamline Burbn into a photo-only, mobile-focused service. "The iPhone was so new, and people were creating really cool stuff and creating new behaviors," Kevin says. "It was an opportunity to create a new type of service, a social network that wasn't based on a computer but the computer in your hand."

They wanted to simplify Burbn by focusing the app on only one purpose.

Kevin says "It was really difficult to decide to start from scratch, but we went out on a limb, and basically cut everything in the Burbn app except for its photo, comment, and like capabilities"

They brainstormed many names for the new product and it took about a week for them to finalize a name.

They settled on the name, Instagram, as a mixture of "instant" and "telegram." "It also sounded camera-y," Kevin says.

For the next eight weeks, Kevin and Mike methodically stripped down Burbn and worked day and night to perfect Instagram. Mike designed the Apple iOS software while Kevin worked on the back-end code. The prototype was basically an iPhone camera app with social and commenting functions.

When they completed the app, neither of them were excited about what they had built.

But a few close friends downloaded and were testing it out. The founders still felt something was missing and were not able to figure out, what was missing.

Frustrated, Kevin decided to take a break. That break turned out to be a blessing, because, that is where he found the solution, which made Instagram insanely popular.

Kevin went out to the beach with his girlfriend Nicole Schuetz and Kevin was talking through this idea of adding photographs to Burbn to his girlfriend. He said that he needed something to help Burbn stand out.

Nicole said she wouldn't want to post her photos in the app, because they wouldn't look good enough and her iPhone 4 didn't have a great camera. She added one final comment "They're not as good as your other friend Greg's."

Greg, Kevin's friend was also using the early version of Burbn. Kevin knew that Greg was using filter apps to enhance his photos and make them look better. He told his girlfriend about this.

So Nicole, his girlfriend just said, "Well, you should probably have filters then." That is the moment it hit Kevin that his friend Greg was using filters to make dull photos beautiful and they should add filters in Burbn too.

Kevin went back to his hotel room and scoured the Internet, trying to figure out how to make a filter.

"I've always been into taking my photos, cropping them square, putting them through a filter in Photoshop," says Kevin.

He figured out how to make filters. By the end of the day, Kevin had created the first Instagram filter called X-Pro II filter and posted an image of a dog and Nicole's foot on an early version of Instagram, codenamed Codename.

That filter was X-Pro II, which still exists today, in its original form in the app.

Kevin says "The funny thing is if you look at the first photo ever on Instagram, it's of Nicole – well, her foot – a stray dog and a taco stand in Mexico. Had I known it was going to be the first photo on Instagram I would have tried a bit harder."

That shot was uploaded on July 16, 2010. On October 6, 2010, Burbn would officially become Instagram.

Back in San Francisco, new filters soon followed like Hefe, named after the hefeweizen beer, Kevin drank while designing it and Toaster, in honor of the labradoodle owned by Digg founder Kevin Rose.

They shared the new app with friends, tested it in beta mode, and kept fixing bugs. One bug, for example, would make the app crash on a user's phone if their password contained an "@" symbol. Another decision, to use 11 filters, was pared down from a batch of more than 30 filters.

They designed Instagram in such a way that it gives low-quality camera phone pics a hip, retro feel. One tap on the touch-screen and an average sunset changes into a tropical postcard.

Decisions like these were made with "No rhyme or reason, just lots of experimentation and feedback from beta users," Kevin says. It was, essentially, crunch time.

The purpose was to perfect the product, but also to get it launched as quickly as possible. Finally, that day arrived.

At 12:15 a.m., on October 6, 2010, Instagram went live on the Apple app store and they also tweeted about the new app. Mike Krieger jokingly says, that the app, which took barely eight weeks to build, was a year in the making. This was the moment they had been waiting for.

Press coverage followed right away, much of it from blogs that had written about Kevin when his app was called Burbn.

Kevin says "We took a very basic action that everyone does in the world, taking a photo, and we put some meaning behind it, some reason behind it."

Kevin adds "The reason is, suddenly all your friends can see that photo immediately, in an instant. But also we make the photo more beautiful."

Kevin says that it doesn't take very much to convince people to do what they do every day anyway and then do it through his product. They were shifting them from taking photos anyway to taking them on Instagram.

"But then, because of the encouragement through making photos beautiful, people are taking way more photos than they would have otherwise because there's a reason to share them." He adds.

Since they released the app a little after midnight, they figured they would have at least six hours before anyone discovered the app and they could grab some sleep.

But within minutes, downloads began pouring in from all corners of the globe.

Within a few hours, they crossed 10,000 users. Kevin says it was amazing and that was the best day of his life.

The night of sleep they were hoping for turned into a few meager hours.

Two hours after Instagram went live, its servers came tumbling down because of the rush of traffic. Kevin and Mike freaked out and feared instant failure, but in fact, it was the best thing they could have hoped for. They pulled an all-nighter, working like crazy to get the servers back up and then to keep the servers online and running.

At the end of the day, it kept growing so much, Kevin thought maybe they were counting the numbers wrong.

Kevin says "The most pivotal moment for us was when we decided to stop working on Burbn and started to work on what would become Instagram. It was a tough decision, but honestly, I can't imagine doing it any other way. Hindsight is 20/20 I suppose."

Close to 25,000 people signed up for an account on Instagram in the first 24 hours. "We were exhausted, but we knew we had created something different. We had a really good feeling about it." Kevin says.

At the end of the first week of the company's launch, Instagram had been downloaded 100,000 times. Another week passed, and another 100,000 people had downloaded the app. By the middle of December which was about 2 months after launching, the community had grown to a million users.

People loved the way the app allowed them to make their

photographs unique, and they liked the presentation of the entire interface—all squared or rounded edges, bright colors, neat cursive, and tiny profile pictures for each user.

The app wasn't bogged down with personal information or a list of friends and interests; you merely chose to "follow" others, similar to Twitter, and once you applied a filter and pushed "share," your photo was out there for anyone to enjoy.

To show that you liked someone else's picture, you could double-tap it with your finger and a heart popped up.

About the Instagram app, Kevin says "It keeps us up at night and wakes us up in the morning."

Both Mike and Kevin and other employees kept a laptop with them at all times, so they could fix any issues with the app anytime. Many times, computers have been whipped out during birthday parties, date nights and wedding receptions. Once, Mike was dining at a farm-to-table restaurant when the system crashed and wireless signals were hard to get there.

He frantically roamed the grounds for a wireless connection until he finally found one bar of service, inside a chicken coop. He sat there in the bad smelling surroundings and brought the server back up.

About his employees, Kevin says "People don't work in a dot-com because they have to. There are many professions that don't require that sort of time. But people sign up because they want to make world-changing differences, to build something that affects millions of people."

When everything seemed to be going fine, Kevin faced an unexpected setback.

In 2011 when Andreessen Horowitz made its $250,000 investment in Burbn, the firm had also put money into PicPlz, a photo service co-founded by longtime entrepreneur Dalton Caldwell. Though PicPlz was aimed at the growing Google Android mobile eco-system, and the VC firm was supportive of Kevin's and Mike's pivot, the investors felt they were facing an "ethical issue," as Horowitz later put it, and thus duty-bound to honor their relationship with PicPlz, to which Instagram was now, unexpectedly, a competitor and so, a month after Instagram's launch, Andreessen Horowitz announced it was making an additional investment, of $5 million, in PicPlz, and stopping any further investment in Instagram.

They did not inform Kevin about this. Kevin, who had been aware of the conflict, learned about this deal by reading it in The New York Times and was devastated. "Instagram was clearly taking off and we just wanted a fair stake," he says. "Andreessen Horowitz was a big name ... and it was like, It sucks to get turned away."

But unfettered, Kevin decided to move forward.

After a couple of months after launch, when Instagram hit a million users, Kevin found himself sitting in the fourth row at Apple's keynote watching Steve Jobs highlight the app before the crowd. He was elated that they had made it to technology's biggest stage.

"We believe it's the beginning of something bigger," Kevin thought, a few days before his 27th birthday.

He says build a great app, not a just OK app, but "cream of the crop", and it will naturally rise to the top. He adds "If you build something beautiful and useful they will come back."

Kevin says "It was both rewarding and humbling to see people embrace Instagram as both a new home on their iPhone and a new way of communicating visually with people around the world. We believe this is only the beginning. With 6.7 billion people in the world, we're a tiny fraction of the way there, but we're extremely happy with the progress."

"Many people work hard every day to come in, enjoy and be passionate about the work they do. It was a humble vision back when we started, simply to work with a talented group of people who share the same passion for mobile photography that Mike and I do. it's clear we've been presented with an opportunity to do something very big and improve the way the world communicates and shares in the real world. We work tirelessly to create the tools to achieve this goal."

Instagram continued to grow and it was named Apple's 2011 App of the Year.

He credits his mentors Jack Dorsey and Ev Williams, the founders of Twitter.

He says "I've always been interested in social startups. From the early days of learning from Jack and Ev at Odeo, I always knew I wanted to create a business around social sharing and communication, but it wasn't until we started working on Instagram that I realized how much of an impact all those people had."

Within nine months, seven million users signed up on Instagram, including influential tech-loving celebrities like Justin Bieber and Ryan Seacrest, and "to Instagram" became its own verb in the tech world.

"The majority of folks sign up thinking they're going to just make cool photos," explains Kevin. "But then as part of that, they'll start posting and discover all these other users and this strong community. They trade likes, comments, and it becomes a whole new social graph."

Kevin says "Every startup should address a real and demonstrated need in the world, if you build a solution to a problem lots of people have, it's so easy to sell your product to the world."

He adds "The best products in the world have a point of view. The worst products have none."

There were other photo apps that people were using with filters before Instagram. So Instagram wasn't the first to do this. But, what they did was to make it really, really easy for amateurs to create incredible photos with filters.

And another really smart decision that they made was to make it an open network. So you could follow anyone you wanted to on the app, friends and, of course, celebrities. And you didn't need their permission to follow them.

Kevin says "And that hadn't really been done before in photos. If you look at every photo service before then, it was basically a friends-only network. And we were the first ones to really open that up."

Instagram never spent a dime on marketing.

Investors noticed too and they got another $7 million funding from Adam D'Angelo, an early advisor to Kevin who'd founded Quora, Jack Dorsey, Chris Sacca, Baseline Ventures and Benchmark Capital.

Media was quick to notice the fledgling start-up, which had just four employees centered around four desks in a ramshackle office in San Francisco.

Instagram represented a new kind of stylish startup, whose start was mainly from the App store and not from a traditional website and rose to skyrocketing popularity. It did all this with a handful of employees, without an office space and without even a web address.

Kevin says "You can be a couple in London who happen to take pictures of their breakfasts every day - it's called @symmetrybreakfast - and you can gain hundreds of thousands of followers overnight because people are genuinely interested in your unique angle on the world."

Gradually, Instagram grew to about 1.75 million members, and they were uploading about 290,000 photos per day, and the growth did not seem to slow down.

Kevin says "In the past, people have looked at photos as a record of memory. The focus has been on the past tense. With Instagram, the focus is on the present tense."

He adds "Instagram was created because there was no single place dedicated to giving your mobile photos a place to live and to be seen."

When he was building Instagram, Kevin was not sure about many things and there were so many unknowns.

He says "The funny thing about tech is, all of us founders are

20 or early-30-somethings, and, OK, we're growing older, but nobody knows what they are doing when they are 20 or 30-something."

He says "We're all learning and making it up as we go along, in the best way possible. And by the way, we're making world-changing companies as we do it."

But even as the company grew, and the company's funding gave Kevin the opportunity to hire more employees, they continued to keep the company super-lean.

The company still had fewer than 10 employees.

What's remarkable about Instagram, was how little they changed the product after they launched.

Few add-ons or features have been added, and the company has resisted from adding premiums to generate revenue. Instead, both Kevin and Mike, the founders focused exclusively on the core product and responded to the needs of the community with great care.

"In the long-run, we'll make or break this company based on focus," Kevin says.

"We don't want it to be another photo-sharing service," Kevin says. We "want to make big leaps into the Web".

In January 2012, Instagram reached 15 million registered users. By March 2012, that number jumped to 27 million.

Kevin says "Above all else, products spread when they're useful and they're usable."

He adds "Companies that succeed look at themselves as mission-based companies."

A lot of big companies like Twitter and Facebook wanted to buy Instagram. Jack Dorsey, Twitter's co-founder was very close to Mark as they had worked together before at Odeo.

Kevin and Mark Zuckerberg, the founder of Facebook had been casual acquaintances ever since they met at various gatherings at Stanford while Kevin was a student. He first met Zuckerberg and his young Facebook crew at a Stanford fraternity party.

In fact, one summer Zuck had taken Kevin to dinner at Zao Noodle Bar on University Avenue and asked him to ditch his senior year at Stanford to develop a photo service for his nascent social network, The Facebook. Kevin had turned down the offer.

After Instagram's launch, Mark invited Kevin to his house in Palo Alto for dinner several times to talk about what he called "philosophy." At one time, he indicated that Facebook would love to acquire Instagram too.

Kevin used to meet with Jack Dorsey of Twitter too. One night, after talking a while in front of a campfire over drinks, Jack Dorsey and Twitter's then chief financial officer, Ali Rowghani, proposed to Kevin what they considered a formal offer to buy Instagram. The price was in the mid-$500-million range, a combination of restricted and common stock, but no cash.

Kevin said he needed some time to think and did not take on that offer.

At the same time, Kevin got a call from another young and aggressive venture capitalist, Roelof Botha, of Sequoia Capital, an investor in Tumblr and a number of other trending start-ups in the social space. He had been watching Instagram's growth carefully and reached out to Kevin in early 2012, impressed by its "stickiness."

"A lot of hot start-ups were losing users as quickly as they get them, like people who get on a bus and then get off in the back," says Botha. "But Instagram retained their users," he says.

Almost immediately Botha committed to $50 million in new funding for Instagram.

Kevin was soon drowning in choices, Whether to accept Facebook's proposal or Twitter's proposal or accept Roelof Botha's investment and continue to grow Instagram.

Kevin stayed in touch with Twitter until he eventually called Dick Costolo, Twitter's CEO., on Wednesday, April 4, to tell him

Instagram was going to take the huge Sequoia investment and remain an independent company.

Kevin also contacted Zuckerberg to let him know about his decision. But, unlike Twitter, Zuckerberg wouldn't take no for an answer and texted Kevin the next day, asking to talk in greater detail about his interest. "A gesture does not equal an offer, because every tech company is always talking to every other," Zuckerberg says of his persistence. "So, I wanted to be very clear that we were very serious."

Zuckerberg had the power at Facebook to make quick and dramatic moves like this. He invited Kevin over to his home in Palo Alto on Friday, two days after Instagram had turned down Twitter, for a series of long and detailed talks about where the two of them combined could take Instagram with Facebook's massive firepower.

The discussions that Friday quickly led to an offer that was essentially double what Twitter had floated and venture capitalists had valued the company at. More enticing still, Zuckerberg's offer included $300 million of cash.

"I'm not sure what changed my mind, but he presented an entire plan of action, and it went from a $500 million valuation from Sequoia to a $1 billion from Facebook," says Kevin.

Kevin wanted some time and he left Mark's home and he met with his co-founder Mark Krieger.

After he arrived in Palo Alto, the pair sat on the Caltrain platform and talked about what a deal could mean.

Eventually, Kevin told Krieger, quite simply, "I really like Mark, and I really like his company. And I really like what Facebook is trying to achieve." They then decided to sell right there and then.

The next day, Kevin went to Mark's home to formalize the negotiations and come to an official acquisition agreement, which they would both sign.

Their back-and-forth was interrupted by a television-watching party for Game of Thrones that Zuckerberg, an avid fan, was throwing to his friends. Kevin spent much of the time outside in the yard, on the phone to the lawyers. "I didn't watch the show," he says. Rather, he spoke to his investors to inform them of the decision and to get a sign-off.

Kevin also closed the funding deal with Sequoia before Instagram was officially absorbed into Facebook, thereby giving the firm an instant windfall. "I have to give Kevin a lot of credit for keeping his word," says Botha of the move to honor a handshake agreement that cost Kevin a small fortune.

Kevin says "The number of people who have either gotten married or had kids or started dating or just made great friends over Instagram is countless. I think we're the only platform that continues to be successful in bringing people together in real life for these real relationships."

In April 2012, less than two years after Instagram launched, on a fine Saturday evening, at Mark Zuckerberg's house, Kevin agreed to sell the company to Facebook for $1 billion. By Monday the billion-dollar deal, including $300 million in cash was done.

When talking about his time in high school, Kevin explains "I probably had a rougher experience because I was super-tall and nerdy and into programming, so I was by no means the cool kid ... I think that's why our company works. I like to say I'm dangerous enough to know how to code and sociable enough to sell our company. And I think that's a deadly combination in entrepreneurship."

The news of the billion dollar deal rocked the tech world, made Kevin a star, and brought the app to the immediate attention of anyone who somehow still had not heard about it.

Four years after the deal, Instagram surpassed more than 500 million users, including 63% of U.S. Millennials. Revenue increased to $1.5 billion.

Kevin says that Instagram is a visual opportunity to tell your story as a person, a marketer, and a business.

Even the pope has an Instagram account.

Facebook, after buying Instagram, allowed Kevin and his still-tiny, 16-person team to continue working independently within the larger social network.

Even after getting $400 million as his share, Kevin still continued to live in the same one-bedroom apartment and relishes a relative shoestring life. "I think not focusing on money makes you sane," he says, "because in the long run, it can probably drive you crazy."

"Anyone can build a social photo-sharing site," says Kevin. "And in fact many people have. Our community is our biggest asset, so we need to protect that and make sure people are happy. We realize that no one on this earth has the golden touch, and we try to stay humble." "That, and stay simple too."

Kevin says "I really love connecting people, creating communities. As a kid, creation was something that I always loved."

When a lot of people asked him if he regretted selling to Facebook too soon. he humbly says

"It's wrong not to be thankful for what's happened."

Kevin married his college sweetheart, Nicole Schuetz, who was the inspiration for Instagram's idea in October of 2015. He had met Nicole at Stanford where they graduated together.

The wedding took place in Napa, California.

Kevin and Nicole live together in San Francisco, where his sister also lives, while his parents still work and reside in Massachusetts. He lists his vices as fine dining and coffee, an espresso in the morning is his 'only ritual'. He continues to moonlight occasionally as a DJ and is active in supporting the arts and emerging technologies.

Kevin says "I think we discovered a way to turn ordinary, everyday scenes into magical moments captured in digital form. By doing so, we were able to translate photography from being a form of self-expression into a form of communication. I believe the latter innovation is the real game-changer for us"

He adds "If you've got an idea, start today. There's no better time than now to get going. That doesn't mean quit your job and jump into your idea 100% from day one, but there's always small progress that can be made to start the movement."

It took over 3 years from when he got the idea to finally making Instagram a success.

He says " It's a long road, but well worth it."

"I promise you, a lot of it is luck. But you make your own luck by working really hard and trying lots and lots of things."

He adds "People who spend their days creating, whether that be in technology or otherwise. I'm always in awe of people who are artists in their fields, people who understand that simply by taking ideas and translating them into reality, they've created value in the world."

Instagram continued to grow and over a billion people use Instagram today. It is valued at more than $100 billion.

Kevin says "Building new things requires that we step back, understand what inspires us and match that with what the world needs"

2

PANDORA

FROM A PENNILESS NANNY TO A BILLIONAIRE

Tim started his career as a Nanny but with his love of music, he started the billion dollar Pandora.

Pandora had two major problems and their death was imminent.

One.. they ran out of money... their employees did not get salaries for 2 years.

Two.. federal regulators issued a ruling that more than doubled royalty rates for Web radio, which would effectively triple Pandora's expenses and potentially shut down Pandora.

Anyone with these problems would have shut down. Yet, Tim Westergren founder of Pandora kept pushing ahead.

Did he come out successful after these bruises or did he give in and shut down Pandora the company he started .. Let us see...

Tim Westergren had a passion for music and he knew he wanted to do something in that field.

He got into Stanford University and he chose a Political Science major. He says that it was a "choice made primarily because it was the shortest major at the university" which allowed him ample time to practice being a musician outside of his primary studies.

He realized that taking this major was a professional suicide. He knew this did not prepare him or anyone to make money after college.

He also studied music at Stanford where Stan Getz was one of his professors. He graduated in 1988 with a deep understanding of music theory and computer applications for music, and a notion that he could somehow make money as a musician.

After his graduation, he couldn't find a job and he wasn't interested in pursuing a career in Politics. So he turned to another passion of his, which is children.

He searched around and finally got a job as a Nanny, He calls himself a "Manny", which was a combination of Man and Nanny. As a Nanny, he took care of 2 kids after school.

For the next five years, Tim would play piano until 2 pm in the afternoon and then pick up "his kids" from elementary school, play whiffle ball in the street, make dinner for the whole family, and then play piano again in the evenings.

He played piano in a series of acoustic rock bands called Late Coffee and Oranges, Barefoot, and Yellowwood Junction.

He also supplemented his income with a motley assortment of piano gigs including one at a Holiday Inn lounge.

Then he gave up the Manny job and started playing with music bands, so he could travel.

Tim worked as a keyboard player in rock bands for about 7 years, often traveling in a beat up van. During this time, he noticed first-hand the problems his fellow musicians were facing.

He says "I spent a lot of years pursuing a musical career, so I came face to face with the challenge that all musicians face, which was to get noticed".

He knew of a lot of musicians who were very good but

couldn't get their music noticed and they left their music careers and had to get jobs, which they did not like.

He saw something saddening: The artists around him poured themselves into their work, but for lack of proper promotion, ended up eking out a meager living until they finally called it quits.

"I became very interested in how to solve the problem, from a musician's standpoint, of how to find an audience—and, from a fan's standpoint, of how to find music you like," says Tim.

After this stint, Tim started working as a film composer in Hollywood.

He commuted to and from Los Angeles, gradually moving from student films to small indie projects, to finally a couple of feature films.

By his mid-thirties, he still was essentially penniless and in many ways still treading water and not knowing what he will do with his life.

Tim says "It was a patchwork life - long on learning but short on security"

He adds "if you had told me then, that I'd build a 1000-employee public company, I would have said you were nuts".

When Tim started composing scores for low-budget independent films, he began to think differently about music.

He would ask directors about the sounds they were searching for and these articulate, creative directors struggled to find the right words, usually falling back on descriptions like "something like Natalie Merchant, but scarier."

Sitting at his piano, trying to evoke a frightening Natalie Merchant,

Tim thought about what terms such as "scarier" and "darker" and "happier" meant in purely musical terms.

He pondered "Would changing the rhythm, the melody, or the alto sax arrangement produce the desired result? If so, then wouldn't it be possible to create a giant database of music based on its underlying characteristics, which would make it easier for listeners to find exactly what they were looking for?"

He says "My job required me to work with film directors to figure out their musical taste,"

"Over time I found myself developing a methodology to map tastes against musical attributes. This sparked the idea to codify this taxonomy and, by marrying it to mathematics, create a recommendation technology."

He adds "This idea popped into my head one day, and it wouldn't let go of me. I give a lot of credit to my wife. She really encouraged me to chase it. We were living in San Francisco near Silicon Valley at the time, and it was sort of like, what the hell, let's do it."

He talked to his entrepreneur friend Jon Kraft about this idea of classifying music with different attributes.

Jon immediately recognized the opportunity in this idea and they hacked together a business plan over the weekend.

They named the company Savage Beast technologies and started the music genome project, They raised $1.5 million from angel investors and hired about 75 musicians to manually decode the music.

They went about this ambitious task of categorizing 450 individual attributes for thousands of songs. Everything from instrumentation, voice, and melody to harmony, form, and rhythm.

The goal was to point listeners toward music, they might enjoy based on an analysis of what they already like.

Pandora's musician team used a 400-attribute taxonomy to classify music. On average, each song took about 15 minutes to analyze.

About a year later, they had identified and ranked, minute musical details of over 10,000 songs in a massive excel spreadsheet.

Pandora's first technical hire was tasked to create a complex macro formula in excel which would match songs to other songs in this huge excel spreadsheet by ranking individual similarities between each song.

They plugged in their first song, an early Bee Gees song into the spreadsheet to see what similar song it will split out. Much to the initial dismay of Tim, it was matched with a Beatles song. Despite a personal bias against the Bee Gees, Tim admitted the song chosen by the spreadsheet was musically a perfect match. The project worked!

Tim decided to take the technology to the world. They slowly started to hire people.

To make money, they sold music recommendation services to businesses like Best Buy, AOL, and Target.

That revenue was not enough and they were running out of money. He was paying the office rent out of his pocket. By the end of 2001, he had 50 employees and no money.

Every two weeks, he held all-hands meetings to beg people to work, unpaid, for another two weeks. That went on for two years.

Asked about how he convinced 50 people to work for free, he says "At a certain point, you do what you're doing for the person next to you, not for yourself. You have to inspire people, you have to lead by example. We were the first ones to give up salary"

Over what are probably the 3 worst years of his life, he had accrued 11 maxed out credit cards, $500,000 in personal debt, $2 million in back payroll that he owed to employees

To add fuel to his problems, another disaster struck him.

At the end of 2003, four former employees slapped Pandora with a lawsuit. They'd discovered that deferring salaries was illegal, a possibility Tim hadn't even considered. He had to argue his case before the California Division of Labor Standards, which forced him to settle with the employees with the last of his remaining money.

Although these employees left, a lot of true believers continued to stay and pitch in.

About not paying his employees, he says "We were too cheap for a lawyer so I didn't know it was illegal at the time".

Under this dire circumstances, he considered a company trip to Reno to gamble for more money.

He continued to pitch investors for money and after pitching to 348 investors, finally, the 348th one agreed to fund Pandora and invested $9 million.

"The pitch that he gave wasn't that interesting," Larry Marcus the funder said. "But what was incredibly interesting was Tim himself. We could tell he was an entrepreneur who wasn't going to fail."

Tim managed to keep his cool and maintain his passion even in these dire situations.

Tim says, that the only thing that held the company together was the "unshakeable belief" that their idea, the Music Genome Project, was a worthy one.

Tim adds "For a year and a half, I was basically waking up at four in the morning every night in a cold sweat. That just about encapsulates the experience. It was emotional torture."

Tim believes that a "strong shared sense of purpose" is what ultimately kept the company alive. He had a deep love of music and felt Pandora could reconnect and rekindle the world's love of music.

Later in his life, when he was asked, how he inspired his employees to keep working for his dream even though they didn't get paid for 2 years, he says he didn't remember the speeches fully but the essence was

"We all know here, that what we have created is unique and it's solving a gigantic problem. No one on earth is gonna do what we've done, and when you use this product, we all know how magical it is. "

"It will find its home. Everybody on the planet loves music. There are millions of musicians who produce great music and they can't find each other. When this thing finally finds its home, it's gonna change culture. And how many times in your life do you have a chance to do that? That's what this is about."

At the all-hands meeting the morning after raising the funds, instead of Tim's regular weekly plea for "just one more week" of no salary, he triumphantly paid out $2 million in back salaries due for 2 years and handed over envelopes to each employee in the conference room. He surprised everyone and a few employees got $100k checks.

Most (good) ideas are definitely crazy," Tim says, "because if they're a new idea, they're not part of the existing intellectual structure."

Having exhausted their business-to-business ideas and not making much money, Tim turned to the consumer market, where the online radio was an obvious option. He decided to develop a website offering personalized radio stations and charge $36 a year for subscriptions.

Pandora radio ran counter to nearly every Internet trend. It heavily supported automation in favor of actual human musicians doing data entry. Unlike rival webcasters such as Last.fm, Mog, and Rhapsody, it ignored social networks and the wisdom of crowds in favor of expert selection.

"It's profoundly unscalable. Our method is really absurd in that regard," Tim says.

That was also the VCs' biggest objection. They were asking him, how he could use this manual approach given how much music was out there. Tim says, "In the end, the only way to answer that question is to look at the experience itself and to ask, does this approach give you noticeably better results?"

This is the time he changed the name of his business and named it Pandora.

The name Pandora means "all gifted" in Greek. In ancient Greek mythology, Pandora received many gifts from the gods, including the gift of music, from Apollo.

She was also, as we all know, very curious. Unlike those gods of old, who didn't like curiosity, at Pandora, they celebrated this virtue and have made it their mission to reward the musically curious among us with a never-ending experience of music discovery.

The site had a simple interface that asks users to enter a song or an artist they like. Pandora then streams a radio station that plays songs with a similar genome profile. Users can give thumbs-up or thumbs-down votes to guide Pandora.

The genome doesn't work perfectly, as Tim admits. When users enter an eclectic artist like the Beatles as a seed, the system doesn't know which direction to take.

Still, when a user seeds a station with a song, rather than an artist, and use the thumbs-up or thumbs-down ratings to guide the system, they end up with hours upon hours of very good radio.

Pandora launched in September 2005. After a quiet rollout to friends and family, the company had to double capacity three times in the first week to catch up with user demand.

Nobody had dreamed, it would be as popular as it was. E-mails poured in, gushing about how cool it was.

To generate revenue, they started subscriptions where users pay a monthly fee to listen.

Unfortunately, the subscription method turned out, not so cool. Pandora offered listeners 10 hours for free before requiring them to subscribe, but users easily could log in with different e-mail addresses and continue getting the free version.

Fortunately, by now Tim was a pro at, as he puts it, "jumping to another lily pad." He scrapped the subscription model and decided to make money via advertisements on its site.

Pandora's listenership climbed, doubling the number of listeners every month and shortly it sold its first ad.

Tim started connecting with his listeners. Whenever he traveled, he would post his plans on his blog.and invite anyone in the area to attend. Four people attended the first meetup in Austin, slowly the groups grew, and soon dozens, even hundreds, of listeners were attending,

Some have become so fanatic that they've written songs about the site, sent boxes of fudge, and even made donations.

"That was the most enjoyable year of my adult life," Tim says. Pandora was working at last.

But just over a year later, while it felt everything was going fine, disaster struck again.

Tim got news that threatened most of Pandora's revenue. Tim was taking a bus to work on March 2 when his Treo buzzed with a news alert. He read it and became frantic.

The Copyright Royalty Board, an arm of the Library of Congress that oversees radio stations royalty payments had changed the amounts that Internet radio stations had to pay.

Web radio stations are charged on a per listener, per hour basis. Starting the next year they would be charged on a per listener, per song basis. Pandora's costs would almost triple, to about three cents an hour for each listener.

The CRB also added a new charge of $500 a year per individual station, which in Pandora's case, with its millions of personalized channels, would be catastrophic. The new fees would triple Pandora's costs.

"Overnight our business was broken," Tim says.

He adds "There was this long discussion: Should we hibernate? Should we shut it down in the hope we could bring it back up again?" "We contemplated pulling the plug.".

Instead of giving up, Tim turned to his listeners and fans for help. Tim says "It was an absolute Hail Mary. If that didn't work, we were finished". So, he appealed to his fans saying "This is going to mean an end to Web radio. Whatever you're comfortable with, please do."

Tim says "Entrepreneurs in their core team need a salesperson. Someone who can tell the story and inspire people and get pulses racing because of your idea."

About 1.7 million Pandora fans called, wrote or faxed Congress. Finally, the federal board agreed to negotiations and after two years, settled on a lower rate. As a result, Pandora breathed life again.

When asked about this grueling two years, Tim says...

"It's been terribly negative and draining, a real morale suck. We were facing the end of our company. It's very unsettling to go to work every day with that hanging over you. It was difficult to keep everybody focused, particularly our sales team."

Tim says that like a lot of sales teams, their ad salespeople would plan a year ahead. But advertisers were hesitant to talk to them because they could go out of business any time.

"I've got to give Tim the all-time award for persistence. I probably turned him down at least three or four times," says Peter Gotcher, a venture capitalist who eventually participated in a $12 million financing round in 2005.

Peter adds "I liked his passion and entrepreneurial spirit." Call it passion, spirit, an obstinate refusal to quit. It's kept Pandora alive.

Tim was a different kind of entrepreneur, Most entrepreneurs, if someone brings up a flaw in the business model, would just adamantly try to claim they've got it all figured out. Tim always says, 'Well, that's our best idea right now." He was flexible enough to change, if someone pokes a hole in his ideas and if he is convinced they are saying the right things.

After about a year on July 10, 2008, they released an iPhone app that let people stream music. It instantly became a huge hit. Almost immediately, 35,000 new users a day joined Pandora from their cellphones, doubling the number of daily signups to 50,000.

"Almost overnight we became anytime, anywhere radio," Tim says.

Pandora became one of the top five apps in terms of usage on iPhone, iPad and Android devices. It now boasts of 180 million registered users and 81 million are active users. 7 billion stations were created and it represents almost 10% of all music listening in the United States.

Tim plays the piano, the bassoon, the recorder, the drums, and the clarinet. His personal Pandora stations are based on songs by Muddy Waters, Ben Folds, Josh Fix, Oscar Peterson, Art Farmer, Elvis Costello, and James Taylor

In 2010, Tim was named as one of Time Magazine's 100 influential people.

Tim says "Entrepreneurship is not for the faint of heart. I'll tell you where I think there's opportunity: the Web now has democratized the tools of promotion. If you're savvy and hard-working and smart, you can really generate a lot of value on the Web with very little investment of money."

Pandora kept growing and now earns money through advertising and subscriptions. More than six million users pay subscriptions each month to listen to music on Pandora.

On June 15th, 2011, Pandora filed for an IPO and listed on the NYSE with the stock symbol "P" with a market cap of nearly $3 billion.

Tim says "I've never, ever given up, even when we were in the most depressive bleak times, I always thought it was a good idea and would have a day."

Tim adds "My experience with Pandora has completely changed my perspective on the notion of a career track. Having now traversed the entire arc from an idea to public company, I no longer believe that the skills you need to become a business leader can only be perfected in traditional vocations. "

"Rather, I think the important skills are the basic ones and those you can learn just about anywhere. I'm thinking of things like teamwork, communication, tenacity, problem-solving, creativity, etc."

"I don't have an MBA or any formal business training. I

learned what I needed to know by taking care of kids, managing a band, and fighting for work as a film composer."

"I think for many people, the idea of starting a company seems foreign. It certainly was for me. When I first came up with the idea for the Music Genome Project it took me many months to act on it , mostly because I just didn't have the notion that someone with my complete lack of professional experience was the kind of person who started companies."

"As I meet more and more entrepreneurs, I've learned that my experience is far from unique. People take all sorts of different roads to entrepreneurship. If you've developed those very basic requisite skills, it doesn't matter where you honed them."

"So when you start to think that you're too old, or you didn't make the right choices or don't have the requisite skill set... just remember that a 34-year-old former "manny" founded Pandora."

Tim started out as a Nanny and then as a musician and saw that talented musicians were giving up their love of music because they were not getting noticed. Tim decided to do something for his fellow musicians and eventually started Pandora. Money was scarce, he exhausted his credit cards, but was still unable to pay his employees for two years, yet he kept moving. His business was threatened by a law passed by the government music agency. He appealed to his fans and overturned the law. Throughout all this, he persisted and kept moving forward and finally grew Pandora into a multi-billion dollar company.

He says "Be sure to 'notice' ideas when you have them. Take the time to consider them seriously. And if your gut tells you they're compelling, be fearless in their pursuit."

He adds "Don't be shy about believing in your ideas,even if folks around you think you're crazy."

3
BEN & JERRY'S ICE CREAM

TURNING A $5 INVESTMENT INTO A MULTI-MILLION DOLLAR ICE-CREAM EMPIRE

Kids love ice creams. Ok, I stand corrected. Adults love ice cream too.

But can you turn your love of Ice cream and a $5 investment into a multi-million dollar business?

Two childhood friends, Ben Cohen, and Jerry Greenfield did this and built one of the largest ice cream empires in the world.

These guys were simply the epitome of bootstrapping and guerrilla marketing, by marketing with less or no money. Let us see how they did it...

Ben and Jerry, sounding like Tom and Jerry!, first met in junior high in 1964 in Calhoun High School in Long Island. Guess where they met.

Ben says "We were both fat kids. We met in the gym. We were the fattest, slowest kids in the class. We were running around the track. We were in the last place."

Thus was formed a lasting friendship.

So, they hung out together and guess what they had, they had Ice cream.

They went to high school together, but for college, they took different routes.

Jerry went to Oberlin College in Ohio and there he enrolled in four year pre-med course.

To pay for college, Jerry worked as an ice cream scooper in the school's cafeteria.

After completing his four-year pre-med college, he applied to many med schools but got rejected.

While applying to medical colleges, he worked as a lab technician in New York. He later moved to North Carolina and continued there as a lab technician.

He again applied a second time to more medical schools but he got rejected again. So he was dejected that he couldn't get into any med schools.

Ben, on the other hand, got into several colleges like Colgate, Skidmore, NYU and The New School, but dropped out of every one of them.

He finally joined the University Without Walls, which was the most unstructured college program at that time. The idea was that the whole world was your campus, and anyone could go out there and learn whatever they wanted to learn, and then they should go back to the administrative body and prove that they learned something, and the college would give them a degree. But Ben dropped out of here too.

Ben worked on a vast variety of menial labor jobs - gigs as a McDonald's cashier, a Pinkerton guard, deliverer of pottery wheels, a mop-boy at James way and Friendly's, an assistant superintendent, an ER clerk and a taxi driver, before eventually settling on work as a craft teacher teaching pottery and other art techniques at a private school.

He wanted to be a potter, so he made pots and tried to sell them. Unfortunately, nobody would buy his pots.

It was during his three years at this Highland Community School that he also began experimenting with making his own ice cream.

Both Ben and Jerry were somewhat disappointed with their lives and were ashamed of what they had achieved in their life up to that point.

Jerry got rejected twice from Med schools and Jerry tried several things but nothing worked.

They both realized that they were total failures.They felt bad about their lives and were treating themselves as complete failures.

But after some time, they both began to think seriously about how to turn things around.

Ben left the school job and moved to New York City to make pottery and sell them.

It was very expensive to live in New York, So to survive, Jerry started working as a cab driver and got a small dingy apartment. " it was a pretty grungy apartment" says Ben.

Then one day Jerry suddenly showed up.

Jerry was a bit dejected with his life and he connected with Ben.

He decided to move to New York to live with Ben and to plan on their next steps in life and so he arrived at Ben's apartment.

They began brainstorming and here is where they began putting their dream of owning their own business and decided to finally make it happen.

Jerry says "We were pretty much failing at everything we did. We decided to do something fun together. We always liked to eat, so we decided to open a shop."

They thought they would do something with food, because they always liked to eat, plus they wanted to live in a college town. So they thought about picking a food that was becoming popular in big cities but had not yet been brought to a college town. And at that time, the foods they thought about were bagels and homemade ice cream.

At first, they considered opening a bagel cafe.

So they went to a used restaurant supply store to price out bagel-making equipment. This was G&G restaurant supply in Albany, N.Y. The owner was this old guy with a gold chain around his neck and a big cigar in his mouth. He told them they didn't have enough money to buy the big equipment.

So, when the necessary equipment turned out to cost more than they could afford, they settled for ice cream instead.

There was only one problem, neither of them knew anything about the business. So they signed up for a $5 correspondence course in ice cream making, offered by the Pennsylvania State University.

As part of this course, they had to read this big college textbook called "Ice Cream" by Wendell S. Arbuckle, the father of modern American ice cream.

Ben couldn't understand a lot of it. But Jerry could understand this very complex textbook because he had his biochemistry background from his failed medical school experience.

Of course, they both got A's, since it was their favorite subject--ice cream.

Since they knew they are failures, they thought this ice-cream shop too would fail and so they made their plans. They decided that they will do this ice-cream shop for two years and after that do something else. They talked about becoming cross-country truck drivers after they did this ice cream shop.

The criteria that they set down was that the location should be a college town since they assumed college students ate a lot of ice cream and that it should be warm.

Since they didn't know anything about running a business, they found that there was a government agency called the Small Business Administration or SBA, which had pamphlets on all aspects of starting and running a business.

They spent about 15 cents to $3 per pamphlet and got these pamphlets from SBA.

Their goal was to make $20,000 a year for each of them. But they didn't reach that goal at all in their first year.

They looked around and found a place called Saratoga Springs in New York, where there were no ice-cream shops.

They moved to Saratoga Springs to get ready to open up the place. They spent most of their time working on the business plan for an ice cream shop and were doing a lot of research.

While they were busy making the plans and researching, another ice cream shop called Afternoon Delight opened it.

They didn't want to compete. They figured that they had a better chance of success if they opened up in a place where there wasn't much competition. Originally, they were looking for warm, rural college towns, but all of the warm ones already had ice cream.

Ben and Jerry were a little upset, so they decided to find another place.

They went further and further north and the only town left that they could find was Burlington, Vermont, which, was an hour and a half south of the Canadian border.

It was kind of cold there, but there wasn't much ice cream there.

Both Ben and Jerry were working hard and were putting a lot more thought and planning into it.

Jerry says "We just took one step at a time and we did whatever the next thing was in front of us."

Ben says that they realized that the word business meant kind of a busy-ness, which was mostly common sense and a lot of work.

So, they moved to Burlington, Vermont.

To buy the equipment and to search for places, they spent a lot of time looking through the phone book and the yellow pages.

Ben's parents were really happy because finally, their son was giving up the idea of being a potter for the rest of his life and finally becoming a businessman.

Ben says his parents were so supportive of this business that he started thinking, that he must be doing the wrong thing.

They wanted to find a busy place where lots of people would visit in Burlington.

So, they bought a clicker which was used to count and they stood at various corners around Burlington and counted the number of people coming to that area. They just stood at a corner with a clicker and just clicked the clicker.

They just stood at a corner and they would just click as people passed by, so they would know how many people passed that location every hour.

Ben says Ice cream is an impulse item and they knew that they had to make money off the passing traffic. Asked how he came up with this idea, Ben says It was all in the SBA manual.

Jerry says that Ben is very methodical and a very thoughtful person and came up with all these detailed things to do.

They didn't know exactly what number they were looking for, but they did customer counts.

On May 5, 1978, using $8,000 of their own money and $4,000 they'd borrowed, Ben and Jerry opened their first Ben & Jerry's Homemade ice cream scoop shop in a leased old gas station building in Burlington, Vermont.

It was right across from City Hall Park, which was a great thing for them because they thought people would get a cone, sit in the park and enjoy it.

They opened the shop in an old gas station, which was totally dilapidated. It was falling apart and nobody wanted to rent it. Since they were low on money, they rented it.

It had some parking spaces in front where the gas pumps used to be, which turned out to be an incredible boon because people could pull up in their car, jump out and get a scoop on impulse.

Ben borrowed $2000 from his father and put in $2000 of his

own money. They decided to get a loan from the local bank. So, they wrote a business plan, because the bank wanted it.

They both didn't know how to write a business plan. They had a friend called Jeff Furman, who worked for the Small Business Administration in New York City.

Jeff got them a copy of a business plan that was from a pizza parlor in New York. So Ben and Jerry pretty much copied that business plan, except in every place where it said a slice of pizza, they crossed it out and wrote ice cream cone.

When they wrote the business plan and figured out their expenses and how much money they would make, the business plan showed that they would be ending up in a loss.

So, just to show the bank, that they would make a profit, they just increased the numbers on how many ice creams they would sell. They then got a small loan from the bank.

They renovated the store a bit and made it a little cleaner and beautiful.

True bootstrappers in every sense of the word, they ran all aspects of the business themselves. While Jerry was the principal ice cream maker, Ben served as taste-tester, scooper, truck driver, marketer, and salesman.

Using an old-fashioned ice cream freezer, they began churning out all the rich and creamy, fun and chunky ice cream flavors they'd always dreamed about, flavors loaded with all their favorite chunks of fruits, nuts, candies, and cookies. It turned out their customers also loved what they personally loved. Initially, they just served four flavors. Vanilla, chocolate, strawberry, and coffee.

They thought about the cold weather and thought about how to market their ice creams.

Jerry came up with an idea for a promotion that ended up in the business plan called POPCDBZWE, which meant "penny off per Celsius degrees below zero winter extravaganza"

What it meant was, the colder it got, the more the consumers saved. For every degree below zero Celsius, which is 32 degrees Fahrenheit, the customer got a penny off the price of their cone, which was significant at that time, because a cone costed 52 cents.

Jerry was the ice cream maker and Ben would be the taster.

Ben had a problem called anosmia, where he had a very, very poor sense of smell, so he focused on the taste and texture rather than the smell of the ice cream.

Not having a sense of smell was a kind of hidden blessing for Ben, because he had to rely on other senses that many competitors weren't thinking about. Their competitors were focusing only on flavor or smell rather than the feel of ice cream.

Jerry wanted to put small chunks in the ice cream, but Ben wanted to put large chunks of chocolate fudge and cookie dough.

As it turns out, Ben was right. People loved it.

The business was good in the summer but in winter it slowed down. The first winter, sales were dismally slow. That is when they came up with the idea, of giving free ice creams for the next year.

They thought that, if they were in business after a year, they would celebrate and treat all their customers by giving out free ice cream.

They thought that it was very unlikely that they would still be in business, but if they were, it was going to be, because of the support of their customers.

It was in the middle of the winter and they were losing their shirts. They couldn't make their loan payments to the bank.

They needed help, so, they found out that SBA had a service called SCORE, Service Corps of Retired Executives. Since they were a little business, they got in touch with the SBA and requested for a mentor.

They met a mentor named Manny, an old guy. They told him that they would not be able to pay the loan to the bank since they had less money coming in. Manny advised them to ask for a moratorium on their loan.

What that meant was, he advised them to tell the bank that they can't pay their loan right now, but would pay them when the sales increased later but would pay the interest for now.

They went to the bank and to their surprise, the bank agreed and extended the loan. That got them through, during this lean period, when there were fewer sales.

As far as marketing, one time they put Ben & Jerry's bumper stickers on the counters in the store. Much to their surprise, a large number of people in Burlington started putting these bumper stickers on their cars. There were no prizes and there was nothing to gain from these customers, yet they put these stickers on their cars.

Ben and Jerry gave out big, generous scoops of ice cream and they had happy customers. They were open 16 hours a day and seven days a week.

People were responding to a great product, amazing customer service, and genuine caring. Ben says "They wanted to help these two real guys who obviously needed a lot of help." Jerry adds "People wanted us to succeed".

With its 12 eclectic flavors of ice cream, including Dastardly Mash, with nuts, chocolate chips and raisins, Heath Bar Crunch, Chunky Monkey with bananas, Tuskegee Chunk with peanut butter and Cherry Garcia, named in honor of Grateful Dead lead singer Jerry Garcia, the store quickly became a rousing success.

Jerry says "Our reason for going into business was that ours was going to be "ice cream for the people." It was going to be the great quality product for everybody--not some elitist treat. We aren't just selling to people. We are the people! Ice cream for the People!."

Jerry says that both of them had a lot of trust in each other and in each other's judgment. So they never doubted, what the other person was doing. He adds that they have very different skills and interests. Ben is tremendously creative, very spontaneous, very entrepreneurial and Jerry likes to create ice creams.

Ben would come up with all these flavors and do all the marketing and Jerry would sit back and make the ice cream because he knew what he needed to do.

Unfortunately, neither of the young entrepreneurs was very good with money, and they would later admit they had no idea what was going on financially. They actually closed the store one day to pay bills, putting up a sign that read: "We're closed because we're trying to figure out what's going on."

They were really good at creating an atmosphere in the shop that was welcoming and fun but were not very good at hiring people and supervising people. And most of all, they were really bad at portion control.

They were giving away too much ice cream.

Jerry says "When you scoop out a nice, big scoop for a customer, you get this beautiful smile and really warm response. Ben and I, we wanted to make people happy."

Realizing that they needed an experienced businessperson to handle their accounts, Ben and Jerry hired local nightclub owner Fred "Chico" Lager. With Fred watching the books, both sales and profits rose steadily.

Ben and Jerry decided early on that ice cream was a fun product, and so too, should be their means of promotion.

In 1986, Ben & Jerry's launched their famous "Cowmobile", a modified mobile home in their attempt to bring their product to the whole of America.

Ben and Jerry wanted to take the Cowmobile on a national tour to distribute free scoops of their ice cream. This was one of the first cross-country marketing drives of its kind. Unfortunately, the Cowmobile burned to the ground when the pair reached Cleveland, four months into their trip. Luckily neither Ben or Jerry were injured.

In the short time that the Cowmobile was in operation, it

generated much curiosity and publicity and resulted in increased sales for Ben & Jerry's products. As a result, the next year Ben and Jerry launched Cow II, their second Cowmobile, and successfully traveled across the U.S. serving free scoops of Ben & Jerry's ice cream. They continued to rise in popularity.

In 1980, Ben and Jerry rented packing and storage space in a former spool-and-bobbin mill and began packaging their ice cream in boxes, which they distributed to local grocery stores and restaurants in Fred's station wagon, the guy who was managing their finances. They called it Super premium ice cream

Ben would be going around selling these ice cream boxes to the restaurants. And the restaurants would complain that their employees were eating them before they could sell.

The popularity of their "Super premium" ice cream spread rapidly, and the Box-packing operation quickly outgrew the spool-and-bobbin mill, so Ben and Jerry moved it to a larger location in South Burlington.

in 1981, in July of that same year, Ben & Jerry's first franchise opened in Shelburne, Vermont. Ten days later, Time magazine published a cover story about ice cream that opened with the sentence, "Ben & Jerry's, in Burlington, Vermont, makes the best ice cream in the world."

After this, even more, customers flocked to the stores.

The reason for their success was more than just the ice cream. They also gave back to the community. They started a tradition during the summer by showing free movies once a week. The movie was projected on a wall outside their ice cream stand. This became a much-anticipated community event.

Crowds showed up for every movie, with blankets and beach chairs. They turned the parking lot into a miniature drive-in theater. The crowds ordered a lot of ice cream. They all told a lot of their friends about Ben and Jerry's.

They also made a point of supporting local farmers. All of the milk and produce that went into their ice cream was always purchased locally first.

Slowly the demand for their ice cream increased. First demand increased locally in Vermont, then to neighboring states, then across the country, then across the world.

As Ben & Jerry's reputation grew, so did their profits. By 1984, they had sales of more than $4 million, a 120% increase from the previous year.

"The prevailing wisdom is that you can't have a successful business and use it to help society as well," says Jerry. "We added value to the company by doing business the way we did it...If you support the community, they will support you."

Did this work?.

In 1991, dairy farmers throughout the state of Vermont – the home of Ben & Jerry's – were suffering large losses due to volatile prices in the industry. The company decided to pay a dairy premium of half a million dollars to the family farmers from whom Ben & Jerry's got their milk. Against conventional wisdom, total sales that year reached $97million, a 26 percent increase from the year before.

In 1986, New York City was suffering the effects of the October 19 stock market crash, Ben and Jerry decided to send their scoop truck to Wall Street to serve free cones of their "That's Life and Economic Crunch" ice cream. It proved to be a huge morale booster to wall street and also helped drive their sales.

For most of their ice-cream names, they got suggestions from their customers.

Ben and Jerry listened to two fans of Jerry Garcia, lead singer of the legendary Grateful Dead band. They named the ice cream Cherry Garcia.

The suggestion for their "Chunky Monkey" banana ice cream flavor, with walnuts and chocolate chunks, also came from a customer from New Hampshire.

They continued to grow until they hit a major problem.

In 1984, big business came after these little guys. Pillsbury, the million dollar company behind Haagen-Dazs, began to feel threatened by the rapid growth of Ben & Jerry's. In an attempt to shut down the young upstarts, Pillsbury gave Ben & Jerry's distributors throughout Boston an ultimatum: sell Hagen-Dazs or sell Ben & Jerry's, but not both.

Ben and Jerry were not about to let this corporate giant shut them down.

They started a legal case, but they soon realized that they can't fight them, because they were so enormous.

After finding little hope in their legal options, the two decided to take matters into their own hands. Together, they launched the now famous "What's the doughboy afraid of?" campaign.

They decided to go after the Pillsbury Doughboy, which was the most beloved food mascot in the country, the pudgy, little Doughboy from Pillsbury ads.

Jerry went to Minneapolis to the Pillsbury world headquarters. He formed a one-person picket line. His sign said, what's the Doughboy afraid of? It was a hand-lettered sign. And Jerry had never really done anything like this before. He handed out pamphlets that read, "What's the doughboy afraid of?"

Nobody at Pillsbury headquarters had any idea what Jerry was doing there, and they ignored him. Ben and Jerry went back and rethought their strategy.

They then placed advertisements on the sides of buses and rented banner planes for flying around major sporting events. Ben and Jerry did whatever they could think of to gain support for their little business.

They took out a classified ad in Rolling Stone magazine asking readers to "help two Vermont hippies fight the giant Pillsbury Corporation."

Later that year, Ben and Jerry came up with the idea of putting a 1-800 number on every pint of Ben & Jerry's ice cream.

"We started getting like a hundred calls a night," recalls Jerry, "most of them between the hours of midnight and 3 a.m." Many callers even offered to form gangs of Doughboy busters.

The two of them were working on their business and had to work on this campaign too. They were constantly working all the time and were exhausted.

Jerry says that in this particular case, it was a matter of survival. "This was like you're either going to get shut down and you can't get your ice cream out to people or you do whatever you can to get it out there to people."

Public interest and media attention surrounding the issue began to grow, most of which portrayed Pillsbury in a negative light, Here was this evil corporate giant trying to put two young hippies out of business. Eventually, all of the bad press forced Pillsbury to pull back.

Today, the story of Ben & Jerry's serves as an inspiration. Two regular guys with a dream who fought for that dream. They didn't give up after realizing that their legal options were few and far between.

Instead, using creativity, Ben and Jerry, these little guys fought back and came up with their own solution to the problem.

By rallying people around their cause, the two were able to successfully take on their big well-financed opponent Pillsbury.

But as their company soared, both men began to suffer a crisis of conscience. They somehow felt that their focus was on money making and they did not like it.

Jerry went into "retirement." Ben also realized that he was no longer an ice cream man but a businessman.

Jerry says that they never really saw themselves as bosses. From early on, they were scooping ice cream right next to everybody else, who was scooping ice cream.

They were mopping the floors at night. And they didn't have a boss mentality, rather they had a good worker mentality. Jerry says that Ben is the most anti-authoritarian person he has ever come across.

This was the time when Ben and Jerry both turned around and looked at themselves and said to each other that they were not ice cream men anymore. They were spending their time being bosses and hiring and firing people.

And so much of what they were doing was in order to pay their loans back to the bank. They felt like they were becoming just another cog in this economic machine. They decided to sell their business. So they actually put it up for sale.

As luck would have it, Ben ran into this older restaurateur Maurice, that he had come to know in the same town. When Ben told him that they were planning to sell the business, he was surprised and asked him how they could possibly do that. He told Ben, that the business was their baby and it had so much potential ahead of it.

Ben told him frustratingly, that businesses exploit the community, exploits its employees and exploits the environment.

Maurice, the older restaurateur questioned him and asked him, why they can't do it differently.

Ben thought about it and decided to turn the situation around, so that he and his friend, could be proud to say that, they were the businessmen behind Ben & Jerry's.

And that was when they decided to conduct this experiment to see if it was possible to use business as a tool for improving the quality of life for people as opposed to making people's lives worse.

At first, they simply returned some of their profits to the Vermont community by sponsoring local concerts and film festivals and giving away tons of free ice cream at charity events.

Then in 1985, Jerry came out of retirement to oversee the newly established Ben & Jerry's Foundation, which donates 7.5

percent of the company's pre-tax profits to nonprofit charities nationwide.

Ben came to the conclusion that expansion was not inherently a bad thing, provided it was accompanied by efforts to use the resulting profits for the public good.

They then started daycare for their employees, provided college tuition aid and a bunch of other things like profit-sharing.

They also used their business to address social issues too.

One project they took up was to work with Greyston Bakery, an ingredient supplier who was also driven by a social mission of providing employment opportunities for formerly unemployable people. They employed former prisoners to make brownies in this bakery in New York.

And that was a very good example of how Ben & Jerry demonstrated that it's possible to make a profit and address social problems at the same time.

Jerry says "If you open up the mind, the opportunity to address both profits and social conditions are limitless."

Following this new policy, which Ben dubbed "Caring Capitalism," Ben & Jerry's continued to grow and expand, soaring to an incredible $132 million in sales by the end of 1992.

Ben as the company chairman, concentrated on what he calls "the fun stuff," such as developing new ice cream flavors.

Asked for advice about starting a business,

Jerry says "I would suggest starting small, and pick something that you are really passionate about."

In their quest to initiate ingenious ways to improve the quality of life for a broad community, they have launched flavors such as Chocolate Fudge Brownie, which contains brownies made by homeless and unemployed workers in Yonkers, New York.

Wild Maine Blueberry, made with blueberries harvested by Passamaquoddy Indians; and Rainforest Crunch, for which the company buys Brazil nuts collected in the Amazon rainforest by indigenous peoples, thereby providing an economically viable alternative to deforestation. In addition, 60 percent of the profits from that flavor go to environmental groups dedicated to preserving the Amazon rainforest.

On May 5, 1979, they started a ritual called "Free cone day". that is still there today as a 'thank you' to their customers.

On free cone day every year, all Ben & Jerry's franchisees give away ice cream at their shops all day. The line goes fast because there's no money being exchanged. You can get online as many times as you want.

Jerry says "Business has a responsibility to give back to the community from which it draws its support"

Today Ben & Jerry makes more than $500 million in revenue and had expanded their bright and multicolor painted stores to Russia, England, Singapore, and many other countries throughout the world.

Ben says many times he felt that the experience at Ben and Jerry's was like falling down the side of a cliff trying to grab onto whatever branch was there that he can hold onto.

He adds that in that situation, falling down the side of a cliff, grabbing onto branches, you're not really thinking about, well, am I having a good time or not.

Ben adds, "But, you know, you're energized. You're using all the skills you have. You're doing everything you can to save your life. And it's really interesting. It's a peak experience."

Jerry says "We measured our success not just by how much money we made, but by how much we contributed to the community. It was a two-part bottom line."

Ben and Jerry started with a small ice cream shop in Burlington. Their first store did not have much sales and they were not able to pay their bank loan. They came out of this crisis but then Pillsbury, the giant company threatened them to wipe their business off. Realizing that they can't win with lawyers, they took their plea to the public, who loved their ice creams. They finally won.

The story of Ben & Jerry's serves as an inspiration to bootstrappers like us. Through nothing but imagination and passion, two hippie youths who were disenchanted with their jobs became two of the most famous and multi-million entrepreneurs in the world. From a dingy single shop, they grew it to an international brand with more than $500 million in sales.

They had fun, fought back their problems using their imaginations and genuinely cared to make their customers lives delightful and joyful.

Jerry says "Don't just do something because it's a trendy idea and will make you a lot of money. The reason I say that is because any kind of venture involves going through difficult times. If you're doing something you are passionate about and really believe in, then that will carry you through."

Jerry says "If it's not fun, why do it?"

4
CHEESE CAKE FACTORY

FAILED MUSICIAN TO STARTING A BILLION-DOLLAR RESTAURANT EMPIRE

David Overton set aside his dreams of becoming a professional drummer in the 1970s to help his parents with their struggling wholesale cheesecake business.

He helped them open a small restaurant and today it has become a global phenomenon adored by NBA players and celebrities with sales exceeding a billion dollars. Its beginnings, meanwhile, are a classic American underdog tale.

David Overton grew up in Detroit. When he was growing up in the 1950s, his father, Oscar Overton, managed retail stores. His mother always wanted to start a business but couldn't.

One time David's mother was browsing the newspaper and found a cheesecake recipe. She modified it a little bit and made her own cheesecake. Once, her husband, David's father gave one of her cheesecakes to his boss. He liked it so much that he asked if she could make 12 cheesecakes that he could give to friends as Christmas gifts.

That gave her the idea of going into business. She and her husband rented a small store and started making cheesecakes and delivered to restaurants. It was not easy and they were not making much money.

When David and his sister got old enough to go to school, she didn't want them to be alone in the house. So, she decided to shift her store to her house.

She took all of her equipment from the store and moved it into her basement in her home. For the next 25 years, she made cheesecakes in Detroit out of her basement. She made cheesecakes in the basement during the day, and in the evening, David's father used to deliver them to the two restaurants in town. David, her son got a penny per box for folding the cake boxes.

David loved music and started playing drums professionally at the age of 15. He joined a band and made some money. That money helped him put himself through college at Wayne State University in Detroit.

He always wanted to move out of Detroit. So, in 1967, he went on to UC Hastings College of Law in San Francisco but he dropped out during his first year to pursue a career as a musician. He then started playing in local clubs.

His parents wanted to live closer to him and since Los Angeles was bigger than San Francisco, he convinced them, that there was an opportunity in Los Angeles for their cheesecakes. He told them that LA was bigger and was more open and it had more delis to which they could supply cheesecakes.

So in 1972 his parents sold their house in Michigan and paid all their debts. After paying off their debts, they had about $10,000 left. They took this money, left Detroit and drove across the country with David's sister and arrived in LA.

Once they came to LA, they started a small wholesale cheesecake business in North Hollywood.

His father would get in his car and go door-to-door and just try to sell cheesecakes to restaurants. David always felt they were operating like a tiny mom-and-pop business.

Meanwhile, David's career was not going so well. At 27, he'd had enough of the music game.

He decided to stop if he wasn't going to be in a very famous rock 'n' roll band.

"I always felt I was good at business. The band I was in, I always took the business role," he says.

When he realized he wasn't going to be a rock star, he decided to move to L.A. to help his parents. It was 1975, and he found that his parents made the best cheesecakes, but the business wasn't progressing fast enough and not making much money.

At that point, the Cheesecake Factory, as they called it, produced more than 20 kinds of cakes and other desserts to sell to restaurants and other wholesale accounts.

His father used to get in his car, cold-called some restaurants, and went from restaurant to restaurant and tried to sell their cheesecakes. After moving from San Francisco to L.A, David started to help them.

David found that, even though they had delicious Cheesecakes, they had a tough time persuading restaurants to take more than one or two flavors.

But he found that people loved their cheesecakes. So, he hit upon the idea of taking these cheesecakes directly to consumers and stop catering to just restaurants.

He thought that if he opened a restaurant, he would be able to sell these fabulous cheesecakes directly to consumers himself.

So he decided to open his own restaurant in Beverly Hills that would also sell salads, hamburgers, and other entrees, but the cheesecakes would be promoted as the main dish.

"I chose Beverly Hills for our first location to give the cake the reputation it deserved, " he says.

David took comparative religion studies in college. Although he was raised as Jewish, he loved saint Sufi and took a liking to the saint's teachings. This had a major influence on how he treated his customers at his restaurants and his employees.

The problem was David did not have the money to start a restaurant.

So, he continued to help his parents run the cheesecake delivery, but he wanted to create new desserts in addition to the ones his mom was making.

Since he couldn't find new desserts by himself, he wanted to find someone who could help him discover new desserts and also test bake them. He kept looking for this person.

Luckily he met this person through an unlikely source.

Linda Candioty the future VP of guest experience at The cheesecake factory, started her career as a cook. When she was in her early 20's she was in between jobs. One time she came back from a trip to Mexico City, and she decided to have a Mexican fiesta party in her house just for fun, and a friend of her told her about a new friend of hers who had moved from San Francisco and if she can bring him to the party. Linda asked her to bring him.

David came to the party and he loved the food cooked by Linda. David thought she could help him test his new desserts, as his mom did not have the time to come up with new dessert recipes.

Since Linda cooked a great meal, he asked her if she wanted to help him test bake new dessert recipes. She readily agreed.

The biggest and popular dessert in the LA area at that time was the chocolate mousse pie. There was a company called La Mousse which was making a beautiful pie, and David and Linda decided to sell a chocolate mousse because it was the hip thing to add.

David says "We haven't changed the recipe of my mother. We just make new ones with new things inside: flavors. We just try to make it as good as she did. You can't patent it. Good cheesecake is just five ingredients. It's just how you mix them."

Linda recalls David's mother Evelyn. Evelyn used to treat the people working with her --the bakers-- like her own sons. If somebody's having a baby, she'd reach into her pocket and say, "Here, go buy the baby something." if someone's mom isn't feeling well, She would ask them to go home early. She took care of her staff like they were her children. That's how she took care of her people.

David never worked in a restaurant before, so he talked to his accountant Bill Kling.

David told him that "We really need to build a restaurant built around the cheesecakes to get the word out and show these restaurateurs that if you had a good enough dessert program, you could do great business."

Bill, the accountant already tasted their cheesecakes and loved them. He knew they were some of the best-baked goods he had ever tasted, and he believed in David.

So Bill King said the four magic words, "I'll raise the money". He talked to his clients and family members and he found nine investors who invested a total of $125,000 in David's restaurant.

This money was not enough, so he applied for a small loan from a bank. Since they had an existing business, and even though it didn't make much money, the bank agreed to provide the loan.

Beverly Hills already had upscale dining, so they developed a menu of casual items around the cakes. He didn't want to worry about a chef walking out on him, so he made up the first menu with things that were simple enough to cook by himself like macaroni and cheese.

On Feb. 25, 1978, they opened their restaurant with no sign or grand opening. It was a very simple cafe. Still, people lined up outside. Linda went outside and chatted with everybody while they were waiting in line, and people were excited. They were not sure what food they would have in the restaurant but they were curious to know.

On the first day, they were so nervous. They decided they would open at 2 p.m, thinking it wouldn't be very busy. But a half hour before they opened, there was a line of customers all the way to the next store.

After they opened the doors, the restaurant was full in 10 minutes and customers had to wait.

They had 12 varieties of Cheese Cakes. David says "There was no marketing. We don't know why it hit the way it did. Maybe it was the name."

For the Location, David was very particular that it has to be in Beverly Hills.

David was very lucky, His realtor knew somebody who had just bought a building on Beverly Drive. It was 3,200 square feet and could seat 78 people and It was the size he wanted.

"It was right on the right block. I wanted Beverly Drive, and I got it," he says.

Every item on the menu was named after all the friends and relatives who helped him.

Evelyn was his mom. Renee was his sister, Marshall was his dentist who gave some money to start.

At first, David didn't want to call it the Cheesecake Factory. He didn't want people to be confused. But in the end, he thought about how he was doing all this to help sell his parents' cakes. Even though it was an unusual name, it helped somehow. It caught people's attention.

"I never really liked the name. My parents named their business The Cheesecake Factory, and in the end, I just kept it. But something about it—somebody was watching over me, whatever it was. Literally in ten minutes... every seat was full, and it just kept on going." he says.

"I didn't know any tricks, and I didn't know any shortcuts. In a very small space, we just figured out how to do it," he adds.

Initially, he wanted to target the rich people and that was the reason he opened in Beverly Hills as this place had a small group of eateries frequented by Los Angeles's rich and famous, like Wolfgang Puck's groundbreaking Spago's.

These restaurants served the rich and discouraged others from coming to their restaurants but David focused on approachability and a family atmosphere and encouraged anyone to come and eat at his restaurant.

The beauty was while the other upscale restaurants focused on specialty items, which can be prepared only there, the cheesecake factory focused on everyday items which people already loved.

He coined the phrase "upscale casual dining." And with the development of the food, the money they put into the decor, it became upscale casual dining, where for the most part, if you had more money and want to enjoy everyday items, you would come to Cheesecake Factory.

Even though they were very busy, the first year it was very difficult financially. Money kept getting scarce and they couldn't get as much credit as they wanted.

"We really scraped until we realized how to manage our costs," says David.

Before they opened, David thought he had the menu priced out properly. He showed it to some people and they thought it was too high. So he lowered his prices and he says that was a mistake.

His gut instinct told him, that he should not reduce the price, but since he got the advice from others, he reduced it.

But he realized his mistake and he slowly raised prices four times that first year. Customers didn't mind the increase and the restaurant did not lose any money, but he made sure to do it slowly and not in one sudden price increase.

Slowly the restaurant started growing.

A lot of business people visited them to have business lunches.

Linda says "Mr. Ives, he was a business person from up the street. He would come for a business meeting at lunch, and he would come back at night with his family. We had a lot of those."

Lots of movie actors like Sylvester Stallone started coming in too.

In Beverly Hills, most of the restaurants were very expensive. There wasn't anything considered casual dining. "We had very straightforward food that was prepared fresh daily, no restaurant tricks, no steam tables, no fryers," David says.

He adds "People would get off the plane from London and say, "The first restaurant I'm going to is Cheesecake" because they had heard about it. It was the cheesecakes. It just got to have this huge reputation."

David loved working at his restaurant. "I loved being a Beverly Hills merchant. I loved going outside and sweeping the sidewalk outside " he says.

They had this single location in Beverly Hills for five years but didn't expand. Meanwhile, Linda had moved up into a management role during this time.

One time, someone offered them an incredible location on the water in Marina Del Rey, and he thought, "Why not, let's open a second one."

So in 1983, they opened the second location.

When he opened the restaurant at Marina in LA, he was searching for something that could be very special, very unique about them and he decided to focus on the interiors. " It would be a real, identifiable interior. " David says.

He saw a picture of a bathhouse in New York that had a column that was made into a palm tree. He introduced this in this restaurant. He saw another bathhouse another time that had the columns made into Egyptian columns.

He liked it and introduced this in this restaurant. "I always liked the Egyptian era. I started to put that out, and it kind of became some things that people really talked about. I wanted something timeless." he says.

When he was in San Francisco, he loved the Sourdough bread which was very popular there. Sourdough had been popular in San Francisco since the Gold Rush. Pioneer and the other big San Francisco bread bakers have been making sourdough for over a 100 years.

There were some restaurants in San Francisco that had the long sourdough, and they were making their sandwiches and burgers on it. David took this and worked with a very good sourdough guy who was in LA, modified it and called it the brown bread.

He introduced it in this marina location and his customers loved it. Later he introduced this brown bread in all his restaurants.

"It turned out to be delicious, and we started serving both breads on the table instead of just sourdough, and people loved it, and now it's pretty much a staple," David says.

They also decided to serve large portions. "The portions are large because we want people to share. We want people to have experiential dining versus just coming in for a transactional meal, [like], "I'm hungry, I need to go eat somewhere." David says.

A lot of restaurant chains that launched after Cheesecake Factory failed and went out of business, but Cheese Cake Factory survived because they could understand the pulse of the market.

Since the beginning, they would have a menu change twice a year and they always tried to put innovative new dishes on the menu.

They constantly looked for trends and updated their recipes. This kept them very current.

Many diners want food that had low calories. So in 2011, they introduced their SkinnyLicious menu of about 50 items, each with a calorie count under 590.

David frequently visited other restaurants to get inspiration. One time he was at the Peninsula Hotel in Los Angeles, and one of the little condiments on a dish on the menu was listed as avocado straws.

For some reason, he got the idea of an avocado egg roll. He created it and introduced that in his restaurants. It became an incredible success and became a bestseller.

He frequently travels the world on "food trips" and samples a lot of different flavors. He gets ideas and brings them back to his restaurants.

He slowly started opening more restaurants in other cities. Before opening a restaurant in a new location, he and his team would visit the top restaurants in that area to see what people would like and what was popular in that area.

"At the beginning, I didn't know it was going to be a chain. I didn't open it to be a chain. I didn't really realize what I was doing when I kept putting items on, but the items were good [and] people liked [the big menu]. As we figured out how to do that, we got busier. I almost felt semi-retired, and then [the business] started to grow, and then I thought, OK. I'll open one a year."

The first restaurants weren't in malls. One time, a mall owner in Washington, DC really liked them and called them and wanted them in his mall. David really thought about it and he liked the idea. Generally lunch ends at 1:30 and if their restaurant is near a business area, they would have to wait until dinner to get customers back, but in the mall shoppers stop in at two and three pm too and would have some dessert and coffee and some light food, which their menu was perfectly suited for and he liked that. So from then on, they tried to pick malls to start their next restaurants.

In 1992, a lot of small restaurant companies were going public and David did not know anything about going public. Even though he didn't know anything, investment bankers came to him and asked him, if he had any interest in going public. He told them that he had only five restaurants. They told him that it is not a problem and his biggest asset was that his restaurants were quite popular.

He was a little skeptical about going public. David wanted to retire his mother, as she was working for a long while. He also wanted to share some of the profits from the restaurants with the managers and people that worked with him. He interviewed many, many companies that went public and thought a lot about going public. Finally, he decided to go ahead.

In 1992 The Cheesecake Factory debuted its IPO and went public. The price shot up from an opening of $20 to $27 on the same day.

"We went public after number five, which was crazy," says Linda. She meant that with just five restaurants they went public.

With this money from the IPO, they built their new state-of-the-art bakery in Calabasas. This bakery catered to other restaurants and wholesalers. It brought in about $21 million a year and started growing.

"David says "The Cheesecake Factory is complicated. It takes true restaurant pros to operate one ." "All the complications of having such a large menu makes it difficult, that there are no cheesecake clones out there. The complication factor has been a great defense against competition, " he adds.

Although the Cheesecake Factory evolved from a small local restaurant to a mall chain, the restaurant has retained customers like an old-timey deli. Linda goes through emails from the company's biggest fans and develops close relationships with some of them.

They have anniversary couples that celebrate their anniversary in Cheesecake Factory restaurants every year and would send them pictures.

The Cheesecake Factory added two new restaurants chains with different names, Grand Lux Cafe and RockSugar inspired by India, Thailand, Vietnam, Malaysia, Indonesia, and Singapore.

He expanded the menu from one page to seventeen pages and the restaurants now have about 250 menu items including Chinese, Cajun, Italian and American dishes.

They make everything in-house every day. They use 70 sauces, dressings, and they make them all in-house.

David was breaking the rules, but he didn't know it. A key to keeping costs down in the restaurant business was to keep the menu and the kitchen simple, but David did the opposite and kept the menu large and the kitchen complex with many sauces and dressings. "Sometimes your naiveté is exactly what makes you successful," David says.

David says, the Cheesecake Factory could go against the conventional wisdom because people were willing to pay a bit extra for the ambiance and the variety.

"I created a unique concept with the broadest and deepest menu in casual dining. It's a big part of what attracts guests, but it's also highly complicated, which makes it a huge barrier to entry." David says.

He adds "I was never in the restaurant business. I really didn't know any other way. People really responded the first day to the food, what we were serving and the quality."

"It was just what I wanted to eat and what I wanted to make. We just kept that up, and I wasn't interested in doing it any other way."

At the suggestion of a Saudi prince living in Beverly Hills, some of the cheesecake was exported in freezer packs to Egypt and Saudi Arabia.

Entrees at the Cheesecake Factory offered a stunning variety, from the signature Glamburgers to main dishes that will leave the customers coming back for more. After that, saving room for dessert is an absolute necessity; after all, those dreamy cheesecakes were always worth it.

The dessert menu at The Cheesecake Factory will take anyone to greater heights of sweet temptations that go beyond the realm of the divine cheesecakes, with Fresh Strawberry Shortcake with vanilla ice cream and whipped cream that will equally delight, or a fabulous Chocolate Brownie Sundae which is delicious.

David wears his Sufism on his hands with a heart-shaped diamond with bright gold wings on the sides. Look closely at the cover of a Cheesecake Factory menu and you'll find a small, winged Sufi heart.

David infuses Sufism in his restaurants.

"The customers come in to eat and pay and leave," Linda tells a bright-faced group of about 30 new employees, "but they deserve something more. It might just be some love."

Cheesecake Factory operates like a family business. David gives his workers flexible hours and other perks like pumpkin cheesecake at Christmas. A waiter or waitress must memorize every ingredient in the more than 200 dishes so as to give intelligent answers to inquiring customers.

Cheesecake Factory has more than 200 locations, and in 2012 it had sales of $1.8 billion and now it has exceeded $2 billion in revenue.

Shortly after he opened his first restaurant in Beverly Hills, a relative congratulated David on the successful opening and told him that he should sell the restaurant and go do something else. He told David that he could probably make $50,000 if he sold.

"Somehow I just knew I wasn't ready to sell, and 34 years later, I'm certainly glad I didn't," David says.

in 2012, David was named a regional entrepreneur of the year by Ernst & Young.

David says "We don't have any food reviews, and we don't do focus groups. It's really me and what I like. I don't like gourmet food, I don't like odd things. "

He adds "I understand what people want to eat, and my taste buds, I think are of the common man. When we put something on, a lot of people really like it. I trust my own taste buds, and if I like it or love it, usually there's a whole bunch of millions of people, that like it."

"If I love the food, it goes into the menu," he says.

He adds "Critics never liked the Cheesecake Factory", but people do".

David says "My father was around to see the success, and my mother was here to see us go public. It's really the great American success story. You come up with a good product, work hard, and bring your family together to do it. "

From a small bakery, started in a basement in Detroit, making simple cheesecakes, Cheesecake Factory grew to a two billion dollar company. if you think about great entrepreneur stories, Cheesecake Factory is one of the greatest stories.

David did not know anything about the restaurant business which turned out to be good, because he broke the traditional rules and succeeded wildly. He simply focused on the food he loved and his customers loved his choices and came in driving from far-away places and made Cheesecake Factory, a billion-dollar success.

David says "If someone's truly entrepreneurial, I believe they could open a business and repeat what Cheesecake Factory has done. I had no background in the restaurant business but it all worked out because I put one foot in front of the next."

5
HUFFINGTON POST

A POOR GIRL WHO COULDN'T SPEAK ENGLISH TO A MEDIA MOGUL

Arianna Huffington grew up in Greece in a poor family. Money was scarce. She dreamt of going to a famous University in the UK and everyone said she cannot make it.

Did she go, let us see. She later started the Huffington Post. Everyone said she will fail. Yet, she grew it to millions of visitors and sold it to AOL for $300+ million.

❦

Arianna's mother Elli was from Russia. She and her family were refugees who moved to Greece.

After the second world war, Arianna's mother contracted Tuberculosis(TB) and fell sick. She got admitted to a sanitarium, where she was receiving continuous treatment.

Arianna's father Konstantinos was from Greece. During the second world war, when Greece was occupied by Germany, he was publishing an underground newspaper. He got arrested by the German Army and was sent to a German concentration camp.

Luckily the war ended soon and he got released, but he got infected with a terrible infection of Tuberculosis.

He was slowly recovering and that is when he met Elli, Arianna's mother. They both were admitted to the same sanitarium because they had TB infections. Luckily both of them recovered, but sadly, doctors told Elli, that she wouldn't be able to conceive and have children.

That didn't deter them. They both fell in love and ultimately, they got married.

To her surprise, even though the doctors said she cannot conceive, she became pregnant.

Arianna was born on July 15, 1950. She was conceived before they were married. Later her sister Agapi was born. Slowly her father turned into a philanderer going out with other women.

When Arianna's mother Elli complained, he told her not to interfere in his private life.

When Arianna was 11 years old, her parents separated.

Her mother started to support her two kids. They lived in a one bedroom apartment in Athens, Greece. She always encouraged her kids that no matter their circumstances, they can achieve what they want. Ellie had a lot of brothers and they helped her out. Now and then, she used to borrow money from them to meet her expenses.

Eli, Arianna's mother had a passion for education. She insisted that Arianna and her younger sister, Agapi should strive for a good education.

When Arianna was in high school, she saw a picture of Cambridge, England in a magazine. She told everyone that she wanted to go to college there. Everyone laughed and said it was impossible. Her mother stood like a rock and told her "Well let's find out how we can get you to Cambridge"

Arianna says "She made it clear if I failed -- if I didn't get into Cambridge -- it was not a big deal."

Arianna barely spoke English, but she began to study the

language. To her delight and to everyone's surprise Arianna got accepted in a college in Cambridge.

"From the heirloom carpet... to her last pair of gold earrings, [my mother] sold everything along the way to pay for the schools and the private lessons that prepared me for the Cambridge entrance exams and my sister for the Royal Academy of Dramatic Arts." Arianna says.

Her sister stayed in Athens and she too completed high school and got accepted at the Royal Academy of Dramatic Arts in London. So the three of them, the whole family moved to London after this.

Arianna was close to her father too. He was a wonderful writer and he wrote a book about his experience in the concentration camp. He kept starting newspapers and they all failed. "Maybe that's why I'm never going into print," says Arianna.

Arianna's father had a disregard for limits, As a newspaper publisher, he spent two years in a German concentration camp during the second world war, and due to this, his life was heavily influenced by this experience.

"He had the survivor's mentality," Arianna says. "In his case, it was 'I can do whatever. The rules don't apply to me.'" but she adds "He definitely gave me that love of journalism."

At the age of 15, she enrolled in the student exchange program and she came to York, Pennsylvania in America. She had just started learning English. Her accent was worse, but she loved meeting new people. She was intensely curious and wanted to learn everything. She was staying with an American family and one day they told her, that they had set up a blind date for her and she assumed that the guy was blind.

When she went to meet him, she still thought he was blind and was surprised that he could navigate his way so well for a blind man. Then she realized her mistake very soon. Later she learned a lot about American habits and jargon.

During her teens, she had lots of self-doubt about herself. She calls it the obnoxious roommate living in her head.She was extremely self-judgmental and was fearful of doing the things she dreamt of.

Gradually she learned to deal with that voice, and she convinced herself that the voice wasn't the truth, and the voice wasn't, who she really was, and she slowly became a little confident about herself.

In college, after she came to London, she joined the famed college debating society, Cambridge Union. From the day Arianna heard her first debate at the Cambridge Union, she says, she was addicted. "It was this extraordinary experience of seeing people, including myself, moved by words."

The Union, she says, dominated her life. but her first forays into debating were unimpressive. With her thick accent and overly aggressive and dramatic manner, she was "painful to listen to" one fellow student recalls.

Her poise grew with experience and she learned a lot of lessons along the way. She says one of the most important things, she learned was, that the world does not care too much about our failures as much as we do.

After being embarrassed in a televised debate by the late author and commentator William F. Buckley, Arianna says, "What I learned was that no one else pays as much attention to humiliations and defeats as we do. I may have thought my career was over, but others were not as focused on one devastating evening."

Arianna kept moving forward and kept practicing very hard. Finally, she got her reward, when she became the third woman to be named President of the Cambridge Union.

"I was a classic fish out of the water," Arianna says. "But in the end, my passion for debating overcame the obstacle of being an outsider with a strange accent."

In 1972, She graduated from Cambridge University with an MA in Economics.

After her graduation, she worked as a columnist, critic, and a television host. She developed a liking, for the writings of a British Journalist named Bernard Levin. She used to cut out his columns from the London Times, underline them and put them in files and sometimes, she would put some pressed flowers in there.

Bernard Levin was also hosting a music game show on TV called Face the Music. It was like a classical music quiz. They would play a little piece of music and the listeners would have to guess what it was.

Anyone can apply to be on this game show and so Arianna applied. To her surprise, she got selected for the show.

When she went to play in the show, she met Bernard and was very nervous. He was twice her age and half her size. Slowly she built a rapport with him.

He invited her for dinner and gradually they fell in love. "He wasn't just the big love of my life, he was a mentor as a writer, a role model and as a thinker." She says.

Arianna began writing books in the 1970s, with editorial help from Bernard. The two traveled to music festivals around the world for the BBC. They spent summers touring three-star restaurants in France.

Even though she lived a comfortable life, it brought on feelings of anxiety and emptiness. She knew there was something else to life.

At the age of 30, she remained deeply in love with him but longed to have children; Bernard never wanted to marry or have children. They had been together for seven years.

As painful as it seemed, Arianna decided that she must break away. So they finally parted ways, but she was still deeply in love with him.

Arianna knew that she would not be able to stay away from Bernard if she remained in London. After some painful deliberations, She decided to move out of the country. So in 1980, She packed up everything and along with her sister and mother, moved to New York.

This move to New York was a critical pivotal moment for Arianna personally and professionally.

In New York, they rented a Townhouse in the upper east side.

Arianna embarked on a period of spiritual searching. She read the writings of psychoanalysts Sigmund Freud and Carl Jung, and of Yogi Sri Aurobindo and various mystical philosophers. She did dream analysis, explored New Age programs like EST and Lifespring, walked on hot coals with the life coach Tony Robbins, and got involved with a mystic.

"I began to see," Arianna says, "how basically for people to find themselves spiritually, there had to be an element of service, a dedication to something more than ourselves."

She wrote a book called After Reason and argued for the need to integrate spirituality into modern politics.The book called for a "spiritual revolution" in Western democracies. Nothing less, she wrote, could save "individual freedom" in a culture where "the 'pursuit of happiness has been reduced today to the pursuit of comfort."

She was still in agony of leaving Bernard and London. With this grief, still, in her heart, She wrote a biography book about Maria Callas, one of the greatest singers in America at that time.

In this biography, Maria Callas's life was brought brilliantly to life, from her transformation from a chubby, painfully shy girl into a magnificent, celebrated singer, to her conflict with her larger-than-life image. Using a wealth of previously unpublished material and numerous first-hand interviews, Arianna wrote about Callas's interminable conflict with her mother, her deeply emotional relationship with her voice, the gradual unraveling of her first marriage, her passionate love affair with Greek shipping tycoon Aristotle Onassis, her agony and humiliation when he left her, and her secret abortion.

Maria later died of a heart attack, When the love of her life Aristotle, married another woman.

Asked if there was any parallel between Maria's story and her story, Arianna says no. She says in her case, she was just 30 years old when this incident with Bernard happened and after she moved to New York, a lot of good things happened to her.

"My whole life, everything that happened to me, my children, the Huffington post happened because a man wouldn't marry me and I didn't trust myself to stay in London and not go back to him. " Arianna says.

Her book on Maria Callas was meant to be a small time book. To her surprise, it turned out to be a success.

In 1986, She met Republican congressman Michael Huffington and they fell in love and later got married. She moved to Washington along with him. Michael later was elected to the U.S. House of Representatives from California.

During this time, she wrote a biography of Picasso and another book on human's search for meaning.

Michael and Arianna had two daughters, Christina and Isabella . "the two most important things in my life." Arianna says.

Arianna slowly got interested in politics. She became a conservative Republican, was staunchly devoted to it and became a noted right-wing columnist and television pundit.

Arianna at one point was the co-host of the weekly, nationally syndicated public Radio program Both Sides Now, along with Mary Matalin, a former top aide to George W. Bush in the white house.

Every week on Both Sides Now, Arianna and Matalin discussed the nation's relevant political issues, offering both sides of every issue to the listeners.

Sadly In 1997, Michael and Arianna's marriage came to an end and they got divorced. She then moved to Los Angeles.

"My marriage gave me the two most important things in my

life -- my daughters. The end of the marriage was painful, but now Michael and I are able to be friends and even take vacations together with our children," she says.

She made what is probably the most baffling move of her life. When she moved to Los Angeles, she re-invented herself as a liberal and became a Democrat. Shutting the door on the Washington chapter of her life, Arianna reinvented herself as a staunch democrat.

Her first foray into the Internet was a website called Resignation.com, which called for the resignation of President Bill Clinton and was a rallying place for people opposing Clinton. She felt that resignation of the presidency was a noble option to save America from going through an unnecessarily challenging time. She felt that the best solution for the country was if Bill Clinton resigned versus be impeached.

That was really the purpose of the site and she found that much of that conversation had started moving online. She realized that being able to have an ongoing discussion of a very important topic, could only really be done online.

Around 1997, when the internet was in its infancy, it caught her attention.

What fascinated her was the engagement, the fact that writers who were no longer just writing and leaving the scene, but staying there to engage with the readers, and she found that the readers could voice their opinions too. Whether it was in chat rooms or forums or the early versions of what was happening online, something new was happening.

After this experience, she started a website called AriannaOnline.com. This was during the very early years of the internet and she wanted this website to have all her writings.

She would write articles and engaged with her readers. Her columns would go up, her readers would comment and she would comment back. This interaction was very interesting to her. She liked the fact that they talked back.

Her mother too even had a column, that they called "Ask the Aiya" which meant grandmother in Greek. Her mother would get a lot of questions about relationships.

People would ask questions and she would literally sit at the kitchen table and would write the answers in a yellow pad and later Arianna would post these answers on the blog.

Arianna has always been a writer, ever since she left college and before. She wrote her first book at the age of 23. Her whole life revolved around writing books and articles. She never worked for a newspaper, but she always wrote for newspapers and for magazines in England where she started her writing and journalistic career.

She wrote about politics and culture in newspapers like the London Times and was always writing books at the same time.

Her books ranged from big cultural issues, like the changing role of women to the biographies of Maria Callas and Pablo Picasso, to books on politics.

Blogs were just starting up and Arianna was intensely curious about what was happening online. She wrote a column "which was really a love letter to the blogosphere" she says. At the blogger's convention, she was given an award for her support of the blogosphere.

She always wanted to elevate the status of bloggers. At that time, bloggers were seen as amateurs and as people who couldn't get a job and were living in their parent's apartment or basement and blogging in their pajamas.

She knew that it is not the case and most of the bloggers were actually as good as the experts in writing articles.

She noticed that newspapers were not real-time, they would report news a day later, but on the internet it was immediate.

With these various trends happening on the internet, she saw an opportunity.

She got the inkling for the idea to start Huffington Post.

In 2003, She ran for the governor of California. Even though she worked day and night, the campaign was a failure and she lost. "but I learned about the power of the Internet." she says. Most of their money for the campaign, almost $1 million, was raised online.

With each failure, rather than recoiling and licking her wounds, Arianna gained courage and wisdom to take on even greater challenges.

Arianna says her mother was her life mentor. "My mother instilled in me, that failure was not something to be afraid of. That it was not the opposite of success but It was a stepping stone to success."

She adds "I had no fear of failure, Perseverance is everything. I don't give up." "Everybody has failures, but successful people keep on going…." She says.

After the 2004 presidential race, she had a meeting, to discuss the role, media had played in the election. Among those at the meeting was Ken Lerer, who later became her co-founder.

She and Ken Lerer recognized that something was missing in traditional media and all the conversations were moving online. "There were a lot of great voices, and we wanted to provide the platform for them," she says.

They discussed creating a platform, that would be a combination of 24/7 news and a collective blog. That was the beginning of the Huffington Post.

Before they launched, a lot of people, including her friends, tried to dissuade Arianna. They told her that she had her books, her newspaper column, and her radio show, and advised her not to take a big risk with a website.

"Very often, there are going to be naysayers and critics. But don't let that dominate, or you won't be able to do something new and risky." She says.

She wanted to bring together three things for the Huffington Post. She wanted to build a platform for some well-known editors and some not-well-known bloggers to bring in interesting content and do it in real-time.

The other is an aggregation of news. And the third was original reporting. Drudge report was doing pure aggregation of political news and it was very popular at that time. HuffPost was Drudge plus three other elements

These were the main three things plus commenting that were, sort of the essential elements of the Huffington post at the beginning.

She brought in three more founders, Andrew Breitbart, Kenneth Lerer, and Jonah Peretti. They raised about a million dollars from friends.

They decided that the Huffington Post was always going to be free and there was never going to be a subscription model.

Arianna never liked the status quo. In 1967, during her teens, after a coup in Greece, soldiers enforced a curfew at every corner. Arianna faced a dilemma, Attend her economics class—the key to her dream of attending Cambridge—or abide by the curfew. "I ignored the curfew and walked to class," she says. Arianna's mother agrees and adds "She didn't believe in excuses."

Andrew Breitbart was working with Drudge and they brought him in, to work with them, on the News aggregation in Huffington Post.

So finally on May 9th, 2005, they launched the Huffington Post site.

Like nearly everything Arianna has ever done, the event attracted much press attention, but the initial reaction was harsh. Although there was praise for the HuffPost's sleek layout and for its news section. the verdicts about the blog sections were bad. The comments ranged from "a sick hoax" to "a floundering vanity blog."

Popular media like the LA Weekly mentioned that "Her blog is such a bomb that it's the movie equivalent of Gigli, Ishtar, and Heaven's Gate rolled into one."

In the blogosphere, new websites sprang up with such names as huffingtonisfullofcrap.com and huffingtonstoast.com.

Some aspects of the new HuffPost, that invited ridicule, were the blogs from celebrities including Seinfeld star Julia Louis-Dreyfus, Deepak Chopra's cryptic admonition that death was not to be feared.

Another reporter said this was just another "media play" in Arianna Huffington's life in which "every waking moment" has been about "getting visibility."

Huffington was a little upset, but she brushed aside these remarks and decided to move ahead.

To get good editors and critics to write for her website, she reached out to 500 of her friends. None of them wanted to blog, but she slowly showed them the power of blogging and reader interactions it provided and they slowly adapted to write online. She knew, that the most important influential people would not migrate to writing online unless it was made really easy for them.

In their first week, they had postings from influential writers like Julia Louis-Dreyfus, Larry David, Gary Hart, John Cusack, and Walter Cronkite.

One person was the influential critic, Arthur Slesinger. He was never online, but people loved to hear his opinions. He never wanted to write anything online and never knew what a blog was.

One time, there was a speech by President Bush at that time that included something about the Yalta agreement, Arthur Slesinger immediately faxed her why he disagreed with the president and they published it immediately and users read it immediately and commented on it.

"it was really what I had wanted to achieve, to have like an instant conversation around the issues of the day," says Arianna.

She used to go hiking with a few people. During these hikes, they asked her what she does and she told them about HuffPost and her vision for it. They immediately signed up and Laurie David, one of her hiking friend even invested in the company.

A lot of her hiking friends became early bloggers too. Kimberly Brooks another friend, became their first art editor. It was her idea to launch their ad section. For the first year, they couldn't even pay her because they were just using their resources to pay for the essentials and did not have enough money to pay salaries. Kim was fine with it and continued to work at HuffPost.

From the beginning, they made it very easy for people to comment. But the comments were moderated. It was an innovation at that time, they wanted to eliminate as much as possible the worst aspects of the Internet, which was the inappropriate comments.

Arianna did not want to side with any party. She was absolutely aligned. The persona of The Huffington Post was very clearly beyond left and right. They were not cheerleading for either party. In the beginning, Arianna personally oversaw most of the political coverage.

Even though she was aligned, big media giants didn't stop commenting about her.

The Boston Herald sniped in the middle of a review of her site Huffpo, "A woman who changes her politics like Jennifer Lopez switches husbands."

HuffPost was growing a little slow. A lot of insiders thought Huffington Post will eventually fail badly.

Some of the Huffington Post's contributors feared the worst early on: One editor was certain "the whole thing would implode", another thought it was "too grandiose."

In one of her television show appearance, the hosts introduced her as "the beautiful but evil Arianna Huffington."

She brushed aside these negative things and kept experimenting on the website with new features. Some failed and some succeeded beyond her wildest expectations.

"Sometimes, failure is not the opposite of success, it's part of success." She says.

"We need to accept that we won't always make the right decisions and that we'll screw up royally," she adds.

But then things began to change. A HuffPo editor David Mamet posted an article about the firing of a New York magazine theater critic John Simon. It was immediately picked up by the mainstream media. A few other articles like Nora Ephron's witty post on her marriage to Carl Bernstein became popular and caught on with the public.

In July of that year, the HuffPost scored its first major newsbreak. At that time, a reporter named Matt Cooper from Time magazine reported about a CIA leak scandal involving a CIA agent Valerie Plame. Valerie Plame was working as a writer but was a CIA undercover officer.

No one was sure who leaked the news to the Time Magazine reporter Matt Cooper.

But, One of Huffpo's journalist Laurence O'Donnell found out and reported that Karl Rove, a government official had been the source who leaked the identity to Time magazine.

This brought more visibility to Huffpo and it slowly started earning its name as a credible news site.

Meanwhile, Huffington's own blogs were becoming the topics at dinner parties in New York and Washington.

As advertisers signed up for space on the HuffPost, and its content was featured by AOL and Yahoo, its audience began to grow, close to 1.5 million site visits.

All these were enough to give Huffington's critics, those who regarded her as the intellectual equivalent of Paris Hilton, a reason to think again.

Around 2008, they decided to raise money, but the financial crisis hit and the financial world collapsed. Very few people were willing to make investments. They kept searching but to their dismay, everyone was rejecting them.

Finally, they met Fred Harmon of Oak Investment Partners and he saw the potential in Huffpo and decided to invest. He later joined the board of Huffington Post.

This influx of money made it possible for them to develop a sales force, hire more journalists and grow in all the areas that they wanted to grow.

Arianna says that the Huffington post is a media and Technology company. They had a great cms, content management system from the beginning. Dashboards were made available to editors which gave them instant feedback on how stories were doing.

They also made it possible for the editors to tweak headlines and to respond to readers. This made the editors feel very connected with their readers.

This also allowed content to go viral and helped the editors focus on, what was working almost in real time. They wanted HuffPost to be a platform and wanted to give an opportunity for their readers to express their views on the articles they were reading.

She wanted it, to be a big collective blog with both well-known voices and new voices.

One time David, one of the bloggers, wrote an article about returning vets and at the end of each story, he would invite the community of vets and their relatives and friends to write about it. These articles were a big hit with readers. He later won a Pulitzer Prize for it.

Winning the Pulitzer Prize in 2012 was a big deal for HuffPo because Huffington Post became the first commercially run US digital media enterprise to win a Pulitzer Prize.

For this article, the readers would write back, because they wanted to tell their or their relative's real-life vet stories.

"Self-expression has become the new entertainment," says Arianna.

She adds that now a lot of people would rather update their

Facebook, update their blog on the Huffington Post or their Tumblr account, than watch TV.

Huffington Post continued to expose their articles to its millions of readers.

Even though a lot of newspapers tried to come online, they were not successful.

Arianna says HuffPost succeeded because it was a pure online player and they could innovate faster.

They were never content. They were always thinking about, what's the next thing, they were going to be innovating on.

As HuffPost grew, Arianna kept reminding herself of what Clayton Christensen had famously called "the innovator's dilemma". She learned how even very successful companies, with very capable personnel, often fail because they tend to stick too closely to the strategies that once made them successful. This leaves them vulnerable to changing conditions and new realities.

She says, that they miss major opportunities because they are unwilling to disrupt their own game. So at HuffPost, they were always willing to disrupt their own game and saw themselves as a work in progress.

More than anything else, she prioritized engagement. Their relationship with their readers was always at the center of what they were doing, it was not an afterthought.

Another differentiating factor from the traditional newspapers was that they stayed on stories. They realized that one of the things that was different about the web was that traditional media would often break an important story on the front page, or the cover of a magazine, and then abandon it there and move onto other stories.

But at the HuffPost, they stayed on stories, like their opposition to the war in Iraq. That was an obsession. They stayed on it and developed it. They found new ways to keep it alive by adding new facts and new interesting views. They did the same with many other issues.

She says that another thing which helped them was the belief that the role of the media was not just to put the spotlight on what is dysfunctional, but to put the spotlight on what was working.

She says, what the Huffington Post put together when they started in 2005 was significant because at that time it was very disruptive. Newspapers did not recognize the importance of what was happening online early enough.

She adds that, if they had recognized the trends, there would have been no room for The Huffington Post to exist. They left a vacuum into which HuffPost stepped in.

"You have to do what you dream of doing even while you're afraid," she says.

Arianna says that she got her knack for relationships, from her mother. She says her mother was incapable of having an impersonal relationship with anybody. The delivery man would arrive at the house, and she'd say, "Sit down; have something to eat." As a result, Arianna finds it very easy to connect with people. "And that's part of the Huffington Post. I'm bringing in voices, some well known, some not, and providing a platform," she says.

Elli, Arianna's mother barely finished high school, but she taught herself five languages and read all the great philosophers. A follower of the Indian guru Krishnamurti, she showed a profound lack of interest in social conventions. To Elli, everyone was fascinating.

Arianna says that the best piece of advice, she ever got was from her mother.

"Don't miss the moment. This was one of my mother's favorite sayings, and it embodied the philosophy of her life." She says.

Arianna remembers her mother as "the biggest influence in my life. She was absolutely fearless, and a complete original." she says.

For many years, until her death, in 2000, Elli lived with her daughter Arianna.

Her mother, Arianna says, taught her that one should never accept limits in life. "There was always that combination of making me believe, I could do anything and that if I failed, she wouldn't love me any less. It was absolute, unconditional love," she says, her eyes welling with tears. She adds that her mother told her that "You could try anything because failure was not a problem."

In society, the sheer force of Arianna's inquiring mind won her countless friends and admirers. "It's why she pulls everyone in," says her friend, the socialite and author Sugar Rautbord.

Arianna was not always like this. In her younger days, she was a very shy, introverted girl. She says that as a young girl in Athens she had to be "pushed to be social, to have friends."

Arianna always supported citizen journalism, where a common man can voice his opinions.

Huffington post continued to grow and slowly branched out to several countries around the world.

They partnered with the major media players like Le Monde in France and Asahi Shimbun in Japan.

On the HuffPost website in France, Francois Hollande, the president of France was next to a student in Paris writing about similar issues and having a conversation.

This was her dream to bring out famous people and ordinary people together and voice their opinions with each other. She was not sure, if it would succeed and how long it would take.

That was why, at every stage, she wanted to speed up the process, even though it was a loss to her. For instance, even though she knew it would dilute their share of ownership, she took in more funding, because she wanted to speed things up and make it easier for them to keep growing.

To make money, they posted sponsor generated blog posts on

HuffPost, but they clearly marked them as sponsor generated blog posts.

They also trained their editors, to write headlines, that attracted readers. Most of the readers came back three hours later to see what's the latest news splash on HuffPost. Headlines excited the readers to come back for more.

Other News websites, which were mostly newspapers which moved online, crammed all their stories in the top fold of their website. Huff Post changed this and posted only one big headline. The Headline was written in such a way, that it created a sense of drama around the news.

When readers read this one story, they drilled down and read other stories. HuffPost fundamentally uncluttered the top fold.

When they were looking at how to make money, Toyota approached them. They had this idea of asking Arianna and the HuffPost readers to take pictures with their Toyota hybrid cars and post them on HuffPost. After this, they wrote about Toyota in their business section.

This led to another advertising success with Johnson and Johnson. Johnson and Johnson's main cause was and continues to be, to nurture healthy mothers globally. They came in and launched a dedicated section on HuffPost. And these sections became another great revenue stream for the Huffington Post.

Huffington Post continued to grow and they hired more Journalists throughout the world. It quickly became one of the most desired internet destinations. It surpassed 30 million unique views and received 4 million comments every month.

Arianna was working non-stop and crazy hours. Unknowing to her it was taking a toll on her health.

One day as she was working, she suddenly collapsed from sheer exhaustion, sleep deprivation and burnout. When she fell down, her face hit the floor and blood was oozing from her face.

They immediately rushed her to a hospital. She got a broken

cheekbone and doctors had to put four stitches on her right eye, because of a rupture.

After coming back from the hospital, she slowed down her life. This allowed her to dig deep within herself and she decided to relook at life. With this rigorous introspection, she had a spiritual awakening. She questioned herself, about what success is for her.

In her search for this answer, she looked around. She saw, how in our culture, we tend to define success, simply in terms of two metrics of money and power. She realized that these two metrics of money and power were like a two-legged stool with one leg missing.

She figured that we need a third Metric, which consists of our well-being, wisdom, wonder, and giving.

She started implementing these characteristics in her life. Her life and health slowly turned for the better.

She wanted others to experience the same joyful and the almost stress-free life she was experiencing. So, she wrote a book called the Third Metric. This book quickly became a best seller.

"My heart is at ease knowing that what was meant for me will never miss me and that what misses me was never meant for me," she says.

Arianna learned meditation when she was about 13 years old. Her mother was very interested in meditation and yoga. And taught her meditation, but Arianna meditated only occasionally.

After her burnout collapse, she started meditating and started doing yoga again but this time, she started doing it every day.

Her book had 55 pages of scientific notes about the benefits of yoga and meditation.

She added this extensive scientific data because she wanted to make it very clear to the skeptics that, this is not some kind of new age flaky California stuff and this was the reality.

This was modern science validating ancient wisdom.

She says "Now, instead of waking up to the sense that I have to trudge through activities, I wake up feeling joyful about the day's possibilities. And I'm also better able to recognize red flags and rebound from setbacks. It's like being dialed into a different channel that has less static."

Asked what is the one thing, she would tell her 18-year-old self, She says "I wish I could go back and tell myself: "Arianna, your performance will actually improve, if you can commit to not only working hard but also unplugging, recharging and renewing yourself."

She adds "And then I'd introduce my 18-year-old self to a quote by the writer Brian Andreas: "Everything changed the day, she figured out, there was exactly enough time for the important things in her life."

"If you'd told me back when we founded HuffPost in 2005 that we'd be in 15 countries, with 100,000 bloggers, I wouldn't have believed it," Arianna says.

She adds that the most exciting part of her job is getting to work with her reporters every day, "sharing ideas, solving problems, coming up with new ways to fulfill our mission of informing, inspiring, entertaining and empowering audiences around the world."

Forbes Magazine described her as a Force of Nature. She was also featured in Forbes "Most powerful women".

She invented a whole, new kind of media business, one built from the ground up to take advantage of the digital medium, one that beat dozens of richer, more powerful, and better-branded competitors.

Arianna's smile is warm and easy, except for the eyes, which stare straight into yours and won't let go, as if she is capturing not just your attention but your whole being. This intensity of focus has led friends to describe her as "spellbinding," "incredibly seductive," and "like a radiant heat wave."

And it's not just the "Arianna gaze" that draws people in, but her total concentration on the person she's with. No matter how many important people are in the room, says Arianna's friend and an art consultant Barbara Guggenheim, "When Arianna's talking to you, there's not that sense of social panic. When she's with you, she is with you."

She brings great passion to everything she does.

"I honestly think, that Arianna believes she was put on this earth to make a difference."

After a lifetime of spiritual searching, of trying to find a way to feel meaningful, Arianna may just have found her calling. " says Sugar Rautbord, the founder of a Public relations firm in Chicago.

Asked what keeps her up worried in the night, She says "Like anyone, I'm kept up occasionally worrying about my never-completed to-do lists. So I have a quote from Ralph Waldo Emerson by my bed that helps me silence my mind: "Finish every day, and be done with it. ... You have done what you could -- some blunders and absurdities no doubt crept in, forget them as fast as you can, tomorrow is a new day. You shall begin it well and serenely, and with too high a spirit to be encumbered with your old nonsense."

She adds that when something bothers her, she mostly reframes it, from seeing it as a problem to a blessing.

"We are not on this earth to accumulate victories, things, and experiences, but to be whittled and sandpapered until what's left is, who we truly are," she says.

Defying all her skeptics, Arianna turned HuffPost into a profitable $30 million business and built a nationally recognized brand.

Arianna started getting offers from a few big media companies, but she was hesitant to sell. AOL came calling too. Arianna decided that with AOL's backing, she can expand faster and in a big way. So she agreed to sell.

So, in Feb'2011. AOL agreed to buy Huffington Post for $315

million.

From the outset, the plan of the Huffington Post was to create a 24/7 news platform with an attitude, and she achieved it.

With the sale of Huffington Post, Arianna became one of the first digital-media entrepreneurs to cash in on a scale that raised eyebrows in the mainstream-media-mogul community. Because this was in an industry, in which most pundits have confidently asserted that it's impossible to make money.

"New media platforms[like the internet] provide immediacy, intimacy and a level of interactivity that I find especially exciting. Those are the things that allowed us to build a strong media brand in such a short time." Arianna says.

Arianna became a super-successful woman, in what was still, mostly a boy's club. Tech startups and media companies were still mostly dominated by men.

Success stories like Martha Stewart, Oprah Winfrey, and others are inspiring, but they're also still few and were not in the technology field. With the sale of the Huffington Post, Arianna became a role model not just for entrepreneurs and media-moguls, but for women too.

Gary Hart, a former US Senator and a strategic advisor to major U.S. corporations says that Huffington's detractors have always tried to dismiss her as a "non-serious person" but, he says, "she is very serious, and when she gets focused on something, there's usually something very interesting there. She digs around, she works on instinct, until it's clear."

She worked hard and she tried everything. She was an author, a television commentator, syndicated columnist, political wife, political activist, ran for a governor and failed, Republican, Democrat and finally a businesswoman.

One of her friend, who is also a media critic, says that Arianna has always been searching for something. Like Madonna, she constantly re-invents herself from time to time.

Arianna says that she has zero interest in her legacy or what would people say after her death "partly because I don't believe life ends with death. I see more as kind of dropping off the rental car, which is our body and flying off. "

When she travels, since she eliminated a few food items like sugar and gluten from her diet, she carries hard boiled eggs to eat when she is hungry. She finds it very difficult to find food outside without these ingredients.

Arianna revels in the ride. She enjoys her supercharged lifestyle, which also includes speaking engagements, such as an appearance at The Women's Conference in California and other high-profile events.

"I have no desire to slow down. The key for me is to regularly unplug and recharge by meditating, hiking, spending time with my daughters and friends, and then returning to my work refreshed," she says.

She adds "And, just as important, because I love my work, I don't find staying connected stressful. I find it energizing."

Arianna does not equate busyness or influence with success. "Increasingly I feel that life is not about being effective. It's about finding joy and purpose in your life…. Success is experienced as joy." she says.

When she started Huffington Post, it was heading towards disaster and utter failure. Popular media mocked her, dismissed her ideas as trash, theft, and idiocy and wrote that Huffington Post was destined to fail. She eventually overcame these criticisms and to the utter amazement of her critics, Huffington post succeeded wildly.

She says "Fearlessness is like a muscle. I know from my own life that the more I exercise it, the more natural it becomes to not let my fears run me."

She adds "You've got to surround yourself with people who have perseverance and a willingness to take risks and fail. It's an illustration of one of my deepest beliefs, which is that we must dare to take risks and to fail, as many times as it takes, along the way to success."

From very humble beginnings, where her single mother, had to borrow money, to help Arianna get a college education, She rose to become a media mogul.

She had a heart-break, and to escape that pain, She was forced to leave London and move to America. In America, she built a national name for herself, inspired and influenced millions of people, and, eventually, amassed a huge personal fortune. Her life, in other words, has become a shining example of the American dream.

Arianna says "Take risks. Failure is a stepping stone to success."

She adds "When we believe in something, we got to stay with it, even when the world tells us no." "Live your life as if everything is rigged in your favor."

6
WRIGLEY'S GUM

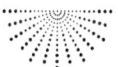

A SCHOOL DROPOUT TO ONE OF THE WORLD'S RICHEST MAN

William Wrigley, Jr. started the biggest gum manufacturing company in the world, Wrigley's Chewing Gum.

He was a rebellious and a mischievous kid and dropped out of school. He then started as a laborer and later on rose to become one of the richest men in the world, with an accompanying world famous name Wrigley's Chewing gum.

Wrigley's today makes billions of dollars in sales.

❦

William Wrigley Jr. was born in Philadelphia, Pennsylvania at the height of the Civil War.

Born on September 30, 1861, he was the eldest son of Mary and William Wrigley, Sr. His father started a small soap factory.

William longed to earn money by himself. At the age of 9, he earned his first money, taking care of a horse, and he got fifty cents a month. Since he was too small to clean it, he was only allowed to feed it.

School and studies were all right for some people, but not for young Wrigley. He longed to start a business, He sold newspapers for some time, then worked in his father's small soap factory, but all this was uninteresting to him.

Wrigley Jr. proved to be a difficulty to his parents too. He was an infamously mischievous child, doing pranks and making trouble in his school. His father was frequently summoned to the principal's office to hear bad reports from his teachers about his behavior.

Longing to be free and set out on his own, at the age of 11, Wrigley ran away from his home.

He arrived in New York City, but the circumstances were miserable there. The young Wrigley Jr. had to take many jobs like selling newspapers and working on sailing vessels to earn a meager living.

Worst of all, he did not have any place to live. At night, doorsteps and wagons served as Wrigley's shelter. He technically lived like a street kid. Since this was summer, he kind off got by. But when the cold winter season started, he couldn't survive the cold. Unable to sustain any longer, Wrigley decided to head back home to Pennsylvania.

When he arrived back at his home, his parents were furious, but they were happy to see him back too. They reconciled and they put him back to school.

A year later, Wrigley proved to have remained as a troublemaker in his school.

In a prank, he threw cream pies onto his school's signboard. The school administration lost their patience with Wrigley Jr. and this time, he was expelled from school.

His father became very angry at his son. He wanted to teach him a lesson.

His father told him that "Your school life hasn't been a success. Let's see how work strikes you."

He gave Wrigley Jr. a job in his soap factory. The job was the worst task in the factory. For 10 hours a day, Wrigley Jr. had to stir large vats of soap, boiling in a huge pyre with a large paddle. This was heavy physical work under hot temperatures. Young Wrigley Jr was paid just $1.50 per week for all this strenuous physical work.

Initially, he hated it, but slowly William Wrigley Jr. endured it and used this situation to strengthen him both physically and mentally.

At the age of 13, he asked his father to make him a salesman, but his father was hesitant. With some persuasion, his father agreed to try him out.

Wrigley drove a red horse-drawn wagon loaded with soap through the crowded metropolises of the northeastern United States across numerous places like New York, Massachusetts, and other surrounding states.

Peddling soap, Wrigley soon learned the importance of gentle persuasion. He learned to make friends through kind, courteous conversation, and, in the process, sell tons of soap.

As a salesman, he showed great politeness and caring for his clients. He learned the value of good customer service. In certain conditions, he adjusted prices in order for his customers to be able to afford his soap but still earn a profit.

For a few years, he continued to work as a salesman and by the time he reached the age of 18, he had some money saved up.

At the age of 18, he decided to strike out on his own. At this time, Gold mining began to prosper in the west coast and Wrigley wanted to take part in this. So he set out to travel to the West coast.

However, his travel soon became a nightmare. In a stop at Kansas City, he lost his money and his ticket and was stranded. He had to take numerous jobs once again to survive and save money for a ticket back to Pennsylvania, his hometown.

In Kansas, he got a job at a dingy doughnut and Coffee shop, which paid him $15 a week. In this shop, he observed his customers. He figured that If they chewed their food harder, he knew they were sad. If they swallowed their food, they were happy.

Eventually, he saved up some money and at the age of 23, he went home eventually to Pennsylvania.

As William grew older, he wanted to start a family. One day, he met a young lady named Ada Foote. They soon fell in love. William proposed to Ada and she agreed.

They got married on September 17th, 1885. Ada was about 16 years of age when she married William, who was around 23. They settled down in Pennsylvania.

To support his family, for the next five years, he remained as a salesman for his father.

In 1891, at the age of 29, he had the urge again, to try to be self-reliant and establish his own enterprise.

So, with just $32 in his pocket, he traveled to the booming city of Chicago, with his wife, Ada, and young daughter, Dorothy, to go into business for himself.

Once he arrived in Chicago, he got a job as a salesman to support himself initially. After a while, once he saved up some money, he decided to start his own business, a soap wholesale distribution business.

He sought the help of his uncle, William Scotchard, who lived in Chicago to provide capital for this business. His uncle, however, said that he will give money under the condition, that his son was also made as a partner. Wrigley accepted the $5000 loan and began operation.

He started manufacturing and selling soap since that is what he knew how to do best. For some strange reason, people did not buy his soaps. He thought hard and hit upon an idea.

He decided to give free items to his customers when they bought his soap.

Wrigley purchased 65,000 cheap red umbrellas to give away with soap purchases. While the dye in the umbrellas ran when it rained, it succeeded in selling a lot of soap.

He first gave away red umbrellas as free items to his customers. He bought large quantities of umbrellas at a low price and gave them away.

While the concept required some fine tuning, this experience confirmed to Wrigley that free items along with soap purchases were a good idea and an effective sales aid. "Everybody likes something extra, for nothing," he says.

When he ran out of umbrellas, he gave away coffee pots, pocket knives, fishing tackles, and many other items. He always bought all of these items for cheap and in bulk and that was the reason he could give them away for free.

About his experiments with giving away free items, he says "I have both made and lost many thousands of dollars through their use. A fellow can't always guess right, but the balance, in the end, is on the right side."

He says that although he made mistakes and lost money initially, in the end, he ended up with profits.

He eventually found out that his free items were a way to find out what his customers really wanted. If they bought more soap, it was because they found the free items useful for them too.

He kept noting down what free items were most liked by his customers. One time, he gave away baking powder and his soap sales increased. Soon, he realized that people wanted Baking powder and realized that they would buy them if he sold it.

So, he started manufacturing and selling Baking powder. Before long, demand for the baking powder outstripped demand for the soap. So, In 1892, Wrigley abandoned the soap business altogether to concentrate on selling baking powder.

When he began selling baking powder, he again gave away many other items as free, such as toiletries and even cookbooks.

One time, he bought chewing gum at half-price from a gum manufacturer and gave it away for free.

He gave away two packages of chewing gum for each can of

baking powder his customers purchased. Again, Wrigley found that the free product, the chewing gum, he offered was more popular than his base product, the baking powder.

He now decided to manufacture chewing gum. He did not know anything about how to manufacture chewing gum.

Wrigley first saw chewing gum as a young soap peddler. He found that gum extracted from spruce bark had been used by Native Americans as a relaxing and habit-forming pastime for a very long time.

He also found that Gum was still extracted from spruce gum and from paraffin, a tasteless and odorless waxy petroleum product. These primitive gums could hold flavoring agents, such as licorice extracts, but became tasteless globs after only a few minutes of energetic chewing. At that time, only about a dozen gum companies existed.

He wanted a good gum supplier for his business. He started researching various gum manufacturers and finally zeroed down on a company called Zeno Manufacturing to be his supplier.

Wrigley knew that the existing gums made with paraffin, were not holding the flavors long enough, so he wanted to find a replacement.

After conducting extensive research, he found a substitute. Wrigley suggested to his supplier, Zeno Manufacturing, that they should try to make the gum with chicle, a coagulated latex extract from tropical sapodilla trees. Until this time, chicle was used primarily in the manufacture of other products but not chewing gum.

They manufactured the gum and found that it could hold the flavor a lot longer.

After this, he started giving away the chewing gum free with his baking powder. At that time, people called it "chewing candy" instead of chewing gum.

As with the soap before it, demand for the new chicle-based "chewing candy" outstripped demand for the baking powder.

In 1893, the company rolled out Wrigley's Spearmint, a cool, minty gum that freshened the breath. The enterprising Wrigley even designed the logo himself on the Spearmint package.

He decided the company should concentrate on popularizing Spearmint, which no company had been able to achieve.

Despite none of his competitors having been able to make a successful go of the Spearmint flavor, Wrigley Jr. believed that this would become successful. At first, consumers were reluctant to try the flavor. Wrigley Jr., however, believed in it strongly and pushed it relentlessly.

Later that year he introduced a sweeter, fruit-flavored gum called Juicy Fruit. Both these flavors the Juicy Fruit and Wrigley's Spearmint would later make the company eternal in the minds of the consumers worldwide.

Juicy Fruit, was packaged in a pale grey wrapper with red lettering, stood out from other brands, and the fruit extracts used in Juicy Fruit held their flavor longer with the usage of chicle gum.

Wrigley's Spearmint, meanwhile, was wrapped in a solid white package. He sold his gums in a pack containing 5 sticks. It also featured a design, that clearly identified the gums as a Wrigley product.

Wrigley took great steps to promote his new flavors. In 1893, he went on a 187-day trip, across the United States by train, selling and promoting his chewing gum in every stop. He continued to also give free items to retailers, who were selling gum in their stores.

Other manufacturers were advertising gum as a help to digestion. So, Wrigley used their promotion and saw to it, that his gum was displayed on the cash desks of restaurants, where patrons would see them when paying their checks after they had eaten.

In 1909, Wrigley bought out Zeno, his chewing gum supplier and merged the two companies into the Wm. Wrigley Jr. Company.

The new company introduced two more new brands to the market.

One was the Vassar brand that was targeted at women, while Lotta Gum, the second brand was intended for the general market. Both these didn't last long.

Since he was once a wholesaler, Wrigley understood that if he supported his retailers, he could succeed. So, Wrigley gave them free coffee grinders, cash registers, scales, display casings, and other appliances.

Wrigley appeared to have a powerful skill of observation. He noticed that customers buy gum because of a sudden impulse. He capitalized on this impulse and requested retailers to display Wrigley's Chewing Gum, next to their cash registers. It became a success and soon Wrigley's sales started to grow.

Because of this idea of displaying the chewing gum next to the sales registers, sales of Juicy Fruit and Spearmint increased and became very popular. Wrigley soon found no reason to continue manufacturing Vassar or Lotta Gum, so he decided to drop Vassar and Lotta in favor of the two flavors.

In 1899, Wrigley was invited to join six other chewing gum manufacturers who were banding together to form a trust. Wrigley, however, thought that it might undermine his company, and rejected the offer.

The prospect of going up against six of the largest gum companies in the country was very daunting for Wrigley Jr. Yet, he decided to plow ahead with his own vision.

He soon found himself engaged in a bitter competition with them. So, he started spending more money promoting his products.

He convinced his retailers to display his products prominently near the cash registers.

Unfortunately, despite his best efforts, sales remained flat. He then decided to spend more on advertising campaigns to increase sales.

He launched an aggressive advertisement campaign to increase his market share.

Unfortunately, he never anticipated that this would almost bankrupt him.

He gambled on two expensive, advertising campaigns, each costing in excess of $100,000.

His competitors followed suit. To his dismay, even these had no effect and sales were dismally low.

The advertisement war continued to rage between Wrigley and his competitors until the 1907 financial crisis and the subsequent recession hit the industry hard.

With the economy in a recession, consumers began to save money and began to cut their spending on non-essential goods, like chewing gum.

Sales began to drop. The budget for advertisements fell as well. Wrigley was deeply affected by the crisis.

Up until this time, he had spent a lot of money, which left him broke and his company was on the brink of bankruptcy and he came close to shutting his operations down several times, but he somehow always managed to bounce back.

The 1907 crisis largely evaporated the demand for advertising. In order to save his company, Wrigley decided to take a gamble again. He decided to go against the trends of his competitors. His competitors were decreasing the money they spent on advertisements and their ads were rarely seen.

With the falling advertisement spending, advertising rates fell and were deeply discounted.

With these observations, Wrigley saw an opportunity, while his competitors were scared.

"They were missing something that looked to me, tremendously like an extraordinary opportunity," he says. But he had one big problem, he did not have the money to spend on advertising..

Wrigley literally bet his life savings on his then-fledgling company, mortgaging everything he owned and borrowed $250,000.

Within a span of three days, with this borrowed $250,000, he purchased advertising space that would have otherwise costed him $1.5 million. Everyone warned him not to do this and that he will lose all his money and bankrupt his company.

"I thought I knew what I was doing," he says. This scale of advertising, he reasoned, would cause a positive reaction among consumers. Striking quickly, while his competitors were still shy from the recession, Wrigley timed his advertising campaign to run alongside a promotion for the retailers too.

He sent coupons to the retailers, with which they could redeem free boxes of Wrigley's Spearmint gum from the Wrigley company.

When the retailers redeemed their coupons, they made themselves known to the Wrigley company.

Wrigley assembled a valuable list of retailers and with the help of his salesmen, methodically built relationships with them. Wrigley implored his salesmen to always be pleasant, patient, and be on time.

When he created the advertisements, his now famous credo was "Tell 'em quick and tell 'em often." His advertisements were short in length and were made with simple messages.

The simple messages of his campaign, and the brilliant strategy behind it were highly successful.

After two years, the gamble paid off. Spearmint became the number one gum in the market and Wrigley's Chewing Gum dominated the chewing gum industry.

In a matter of months, Wrigley had grown his market from the Midwest to the entire nation. By 1910, sales increased from $170,000 to more than $3 million. Wrigley's Spearmint became the largest-selling brand in America.

"I believe in advertising and I believe in advertising all the time," he says. He adds "There is no such thing as getting a business so established that it does not need to advertise. Babies who never heard about you, are being born every day, and people who once knew you, forget you if you don't keep them reminded constantly."

Looking to expand, Wrigley turned his attention to English-speaking foreign countries. He decided to sell in Great Britain.

In Great Britain, however, he found that the practice of chewing gum was held in low esteem. In fact, it was viewed as a habit every bit as distasteful as chewing tobacco.

All his efforts to sell his chewing gum in Great Britain failed, so he decided to abandon it.

He next turned his attention to other English speaking countries. In 1910, he established factories in Canada and in Australia in 1915.

Wrigley started a few other minor brands of chewing gum, including Sweet 16, Licorice, Pepsin, Blood Orange, Pineapple, Banana, and Lemon Cream.

However, he could not spend money on marketing on all these different products. At the same time, his other flagship brands like Juicy fruit were getting more popular, so he gradually phased out these products.

In 1914, fearing stagnation in the product line, Wrigley added a new peppermint flavor, Doublemint. Wrapped in a bold green package, but with a two-headed arrow logo--the new brand was touted as "double strength," "double good," and "double distilled."

To keep the Wrigley name in the public consciousness, Wrigley bought huge public billboards, upon which he plastered his simple advertising messages: "Doublemint, Double Good" and "Chew Juicy Fruit."

After 1930, Doublemint was promoted consistently with twins, double images, and even a double-talking radio comedian. Double-talk comedy was a show where comedians used invented or nonsense words to give the appearance of knowledge and amuse the audience.

One time, he was looking at the telephone directory and got an idea. He thumbed through it and noticed the thousands of names and addresses in the book.

In 1915, in one spectacular stunt, which possibly marked the birth of direct marketing, Wrigley mailed a complimentary four-stick package of gum to almost 1.5 million addresses from a phone directory.

In 1919, he did it again on a larger scale, sending a pack of free chewing gum, to over 7 million homes across the United States that owned a telephone. He reasoned, that people with telephones could afford his gum.

In the same year, he also studded a mile long of railroad between Atlantic City and Trenton with billboards showing Wrigley's ads. His ideas helped, to increase the sales of his chewing gum, in addition to keeping it cheap at 5 cents.

Ever curious to try new methods of advertising, Wrigley continued to expand his advertising strategy to include new techniques.

In the early 1920s, he placed posters promoting his gum in all 62,000 buses, subways, and train cars that existed at the time throughout the entire country.

These activities helped sustain Wrigley's gum and established it as a national brand.

Wrigley wanted to offer stock to his employees. So, In 1919, he took the company public and began trading stocks on Wall Street.

One of his dreams was to build one of the country's most architecturally impressive headquarters. Before any other company had established itself on the north side of the Chicago River, Wrigley Jr. decided to make the move.

The Wrigley Building, a world famous modern-day symbol of Chicago, was completed in 1924.

It featured a 27-story clock tower which was an instant hit in Chicago.

This building construction also launched the development of Chicago's "Magnificent Mile."

Today, The Magnificent Mile is Chicago's premier commercial district. The vibrant, bustling area is home to upscale shops, luxe fashion outlets, cool restaurants, and posh hotels.

The Wrigley Building symbolizes Chicago for many people and has been seen, in countless movies and television shows.

One of Wrigley Jr.'s most admired qualities was his enthusiasm. Over his desk in his office hung a sign that read, "Nothing great was ever achieved without enthusiasm." Wrigley Jr. tried to live up. to that motto each and every day.

Indeed, Wrigley Jr. was able to evoke enthusiasm each and every day, because of the very fact that he loved what he was doing. "Nothing is so much fun as a business," he once said. "I do not expect to do anything but work as long as I can stand up."

Wrigley Jr.'s enthusiasm also proved infectious among his colleagues. "I have never seen Mr. Wrigley Jr. worried," says one Wrigley executive. "In crises that would have crushed many men, that had me running around in circles, he remained as calm, as cheerful as if he were on a Sunday picnic." the executive added.

Wrigley Jr. was enthusiastic about his business too because he believed that taking care of his people would take care of his business.

He treated his employees as fairly as possible. Indeed, he was one of the first business person in America to adopt the five-day workweek in 1924, giving employees Saturdays off. He also provided them with medical care, life insurance, and stocks.

Once, a vendor had approached Wrigley Jr. and offered to sell him a promotional item. A deal was negotiated, but later on, the vendor suggested, he was going to lose money because Wrigley Jr. had somehow managed to get a good deal. "We don't want to do business with anybody who loses money on us," responded Wrigley Jr., who then immediately proceeded to tear up the contract.

His simple philosophy for life was summed up, "To be always pleasant, always patient, always on time, and never to argue."

In 1929, L.P. Larson another businessman, sued Wrigley for using his trademark in an advertisement. They had used the name "Wintermint" in the Wrigley advertisements for "Doublemint" gum.

Eventually, the lawsuit resulted Wrigley, to pay Larson about $1.5 million. But Wrigley brushed aside this lawsuit and focused on growing his company. Wrigley's company continued to grow.

He also had a number of passions outside of the business world. One such passion was for baseball. Wrigley Jr. was a life-long baseball fan and an avid Chicago Cubs fan. Even as his company grew bigger, Wrigley Jr. would still find the time to go with friends to the ballpark to catch a game, and even hand out cigars to the ball players.

With his profits, Wrigley later purchased a share in the Chicago Cubs baseball team in 1916.

Then In 1921 he acquired his partner's controlling interests in the team and became the owner of his favorite team and its ballpark, then known as Cubs Park.

He then proceeded to assemble an all-star team. Much like the way he ran his business, Wrigley Jr. insisted on having the best people on his baseball team too.

Over the next few years, Wrigley Jr. invested more than $5 million into his team and the stadium, which was officially renamed to Wrigley Field in honor of its owner. He started installing permanent bleacher seats as well as expanded box seats and an upper deck. If his name was going to be emblazoned on this stadium, Wrigley Jr. decided that it had to be the best stadium there was.

Even in baseball, he was not afraid to experiment with new ways of bringing in more people.

He was the first baseball club owners to ever promote a Ladies Day to bring women to the ballpark.

He was also the first to regularly broadcast his team's games live on the radio when other owners feared, it would cause fans to stay at home. In 1929, the Chicago Cubs broke the major league's attendance record and went on to win the sport's championship the same year.

Wrigley's business was growing well, but disaster struck again. In October of 1929, the ticker tapes on wall street began to unravel an ominous message. Stocks were declining. America was facing the worst business disaster in its history. Factories were closing. Men were thrown out of work and were forced to roam the streets, hungry and homeless.

Wrigley decided to something and he donated large sums of money to the relief drive. He turned one of his big building on the west side of Chicago over to the salvation army for sleeping quarters.

During the years of business depression, Wrigley devoted time, money and the use of his vast properties to care for the destitute and homeless.

Slowly the depression ended and life came back to normal. In 1919, he purchased Santa Catalina Island in California for about $3 million. This beautiful island was twenty-six miles off the coast of southern California.

Wrigley imported birds from all over the world to the island. To bring attention and tourists to the Island, he made the Island the spring training home for the Chicago Cub's baseball team, which he owned. Wrigley also built the Catalina Country Club to house the team's lockers and provide a gathering place for players.

Under Wrigley's supervision, slowly Catalina island became one of the most spectacular resorts in the country. He turned it into a family retreat and developed it into a world-famous glittering tourist attraction on the Pacific coast.

It was that same attitude of wanting to be the best, that guided Wrigley Jr. in building the famed Catalina Island.

By importing plants and birds from around the world, and investing in infrastructure and more, Wrigley Jr. was able to turn the island into one of the most famous resorts in the United States.

Catalina Island with its swaying palms, glass bottom boats to view flying fish and Undersea Expeditions were attractions to the island that draw millions of visitors each year.It became a popular spot for Hollywood filming too.

Wrigley also invested in various hotels and mines in the then booming and growing city of Los Angeles.

These endeavors helped to keep the Wrigley family in good financial health through the difficult years of the Great Depression.

The company entered a potentially disastrous era, as the United States escalated its involvement in the war in Europe. After the Japanese bombing of Pearl Harbor in 1941, the company found shipping unavailable and quality ingredients in increasingly short supply.

Production of Wrigley's three famous brands had to be severely scaled back. All the gum which was manufactured was sent to the armed forces. The US Army reportedly found the use of the gum helped soldiers relax and revitalize.

Left only with inferior ingredients, in 1944, the company introduced a temporary brand called Orbit.

Admitting that the brand was not up to its standards, Wrigley was secure in the knowledge that Orbit would be discontinued, when the company could again sell its premium brands.

To avoid confusion or consumer dissatisfaction, Wrigley gave the new gum an entirely different package design that did not include his trademark arrow found on his other gums.

Soon, however, Wrigley found it impossible to produce its

premium brands even for the military. For the remainder of the war, the company produced only Orbit.

Even though Wrigley was not able to manufacture his premium brands, he continued to advertise them.

In billboard and print advertisements, the company featured an empty Wrigley's Spearmint wrapper with the caption, "Remember this wrapper!"

This campaign was so successful that when the war ended and the brands were reintroduced, pent-up demand caused consumption of Wrigley's Spearmint, Doublemint, and Juicy Fruit to exceed prewar levels. He discontinued Orbit at this time.

Dedicated to maintaining the value of the company's brands to consumers, Wrigley insisted that the price of his product be held at five cents per package.

When asked what was the single most important factor behind his company success, whether it was the product, whether it was the long hours that he worked, Was it the premiums he offered or was it, his advertising. He says it is none of these.

"I have always unhesitatingly answered." "restraint in regard to immediate profits," answered Wrigley Jr.

"That has not only been our most profitable policy, it has been, pretty nearly our only profitable one," he added.

Wrigley Jr. was in business for the long-term and he fervently believed in it.

By holding the line against price increases, Wrigley built strong dealer confidence in his brands and held his raw materials suppliers to more stable terms.

However, this was only possible because the company dominated the market for chewing gum and was able to incorporate newer, more efficient production and distribution methods.

In time, Wrigley's competitors were forced to raise the price of their products. This won the Wrigley company, even greater loyalty from retailers and convinced many consumers to abandon their brands for Wrigley.

By 1922, the company was selling over 10 billion sticks of gum each year. William Wrigley Jr became one of the world's richest man.

When asked his secret of success, he says, there is no secret. "What I've accomplished has been done, because I've enjoyed every moment of the battle," he says.

On January 1932, the world was saddened, by the passing of William Wrigley Jr at the age of 70, a man of the people, philanthropist, sportsman, and all around good fellow, captain of industry.

William Wrigly Jr, rose from a school dropout, working as a laborer and even though he failed multiple times in starting a new business, he never lost his zeal and enthusiasm for new things and kept experimenting.

His good-heartedness towards his fellow human beings made him do business for the well being of others.

Today, Wrigley's chewing gum, the company he founded has become the world's largest maker of chewing gum products in the world.

Its brands include the ever-popular Big Red, Extra, Freedent, Juicy Fruit, Hubba Bubba Bubble Tape, Altoids, and Life Savers. Its revenues exceeded more than $5 billion.

Wrigley Jr. was known for his courage and persistence. He used to say that, "A man's doubts and fears are his worst enemies. He can go ahead and do anything, as long as he believed in himself."

7
MINECRAFT

DEPRESSED KID STARTING A SIDE HUSTLE TO SELLING IT FOR $2+ BILLION

Markus Persson started the game Minecraft as a side project while working on his day job.

He had personal tragedies during this time. Yet he kept developing the game. He intended to sell a few games, but the results were astonishing. Later on, he sold the game to Microsoft for $2+ billion.

Markus Persson grew up in Edsbyn, a provincial town near Sweden's eastern coast.

While other children played soccer in the summer and bandy, a variation of ice hockey with a ball, in the winter, the introverted Markus tinkered for hours on end with Legos.

When he was seven, Markus's father, a railroad worker, bought home a Commodore 128 computer and also taught him how to use it.

He had a number of bootleg games like some weird Mickey Mouse tower games, Balderdash etc and used to play them.

Computer magazines of the day would print strings of code

on their back pages, which could be transcribed by the reader to create a playable game.

This code-by-numbers task gave Markus his first experience of what would later become his profession.

His sister would read the lines out to him and he would tap them into the computer.

After a while, he figured out that if he didn't type out exactly what they told him, then something different would happen. He used to type the instructions and finally run the games. He says "That sense of power was intoxicating."

When he was seven and in second grade, his family moved to Stockholm.

Unable to make new friends easily, he became ever closer to the family computer, which offered entertainment like Boulder Dash, an 8-bit puzzle game and The Bard's Tale, an action-role-playing title.

Markus's mother, Ritva, recalls periods when her son would fake stomachaches to stay home from school and while away hours in front of the computer.

The young Markus found further solace in computers as life at home fell apart. His parents divorced when he was 12. Markus's father became an abused alcoholic and also became addicted to amphetamines.

His younger sister also began to experiment with drugs and eventually ran away from home.

When he was about 13, he found a group of programmers in his school and they competed with one another to create the most impressive effects on their Atari STs.

Markus failed to finish high school. He continued to live at home with his mother, a nurse who worked the graveyard shift at a local hospital.

His mother seeing his passion for games forced him to take an online programming course. It turned out to be a wise investment. Channeling his childhood passion, he started churning out games.

From the age of 15 to 18, he studied about Print & Media. He learnt about design, font setting and copywriting. His first job was for a small web studio. That lasted about six months. Then the IT crash came and he was out of work for a couple of years. He continued to stay with his mother, since he was not making any money. Then he found a small job helping out at a tiny printing store doing web page development.

Then he got a job at Game Federation where they were making middleware for digital distribution. During this time he met Rolf Jannson. They became friends and together they both made a game called Wurm Online.

in 2004, at the age of 24, he landed a gig at Midas player, later renamed as King.com, the maker of Candy Crush.

While there he made friends with fellow geek Jakob Porsér, an equally reserved young developer.

It was a great job for both of them because they had the freedom to do most of the stuff in the game by themselves without instructions from anyone, except for the graphics. In their job, they were creating lots of flash-player based games.

It was kind of intense. They just spent one or two months on each game. During his time at King.com, he made around 30 games. He did the programming and he worked along with one games designer and one artist.

Of all the games he developed, he says his favorites are Zuma, Luxor ports, the pinball game Pinball King, and a simple little game called Duck Pond Dash.

Markus says "The thing I learned there was how to actually finish projects, which was very, very valuable."

In the meantime his friend Rolf, with whom he had developed the "Wurm online" game moved from Stockholm to Motala. The two were seeing less of each other and Markus knew that the big decisions about the "Wurm online" game's development were increasingly in Rolf's hands.

Markus also had a very busy time at king.com and so, he informed Rolf that he would like to drop and not work on Wurm Online anymore.

Rolf was disappointed. Wurm Online had just began to pull in enough money to give him a decent full-time salary. The sudden resignation of Markus, one of the game's founders, the friend with whom he'd worked for more than three years, was a huge blow.

Initially, Markus had a bad conscience about it. He felt like he had left his old friend in the lurch. They talked it out and Markus retained a small part of his ownership in the shared company but turned over the rest to Rolf. A Band-Aid on the sore if nothing else, he thought.

Markus then discovered the indie gaming scene, where independent game developers were developing their own games. He was fascinated by it, because now anyone can develop their own game and release it directly to the consumers.

So, in his spare time, he continued to work on his own projects, entering competitions to make games with tight memory constraints in order to focus his creativity. Some of these games gained notoriety on indie game websites.

His bosses at king.com did not like the fact, that he was developing his own games.

They thought that he could become their competitor. So, they asked him to stop making his own games, but Markus continued to develop the games on his own.

But over time, the pressure grew more and more from his bosses, So he finally quit his job at king.com. He looked around and found a job as a programmer in another company called Jalbum, an online photo-sharing service.

His bosses at the new company were not bothered by him

developing games in his spare time after work and he liked this freedom.

He loved the indie scene that had sprung up in the gaming world. While it was hard for him to put his finger on exactly what it was that attracted him, he felt at home there, much more than working as a developer in one of the large, established gaming companies.

His favorite online hangout was the game forum TIGSource, a meeting place for indie developers, where Markus, known with the Nickname Notch in that forum, quickly found a group of friends and acquaintances to talk games with.

He loved the burning creativity of the indie scene, its focus on new, interesting gaming concepts rather than on elaborate graphics and expensive manuscripts. He liked that each programmer controlled his own projects entirely.

"Indie" literally means independent, that an individual can develop a game without a large company doling out instructions. Markus felt that indie was a matter of self-image, It was about creating games for their own sake, where the goal isn't to make money but to make the best game possible.

The gaming industry differs from other creative businesses in that the game designers are seldom recognized for their work in the way famous musicians or film directors are.

In the gaming world, it's the publishers or studios that are recognized after a well-received game release, seldom the individuals who created the games. That's because game development is, in most cases, a collective achievement.

In a project with several hundred programmers, it's almost impossible to point out just one person as the brain or the visionary behind the whole thing.

In the indie scene, on the other hand, a single programmer can put together a game of his or her own and stand behind everything from the basic vision to the implementation.

Markus felt that the indie scene, being closer to artistry than it is to systems development, had, for the first time, given the individual game developer an identity to embrace.

Markus has never thought of himself as a Java programmer, graphic artist, or musician. He saw himself as a game maker, plain and simple. The indie scene was the only place, where he could just be that.

He loved a game called Dwarf Fortress and he planned to create a better version of this game. Markus's thoughts were fully focused on his next project, on amusement parks, medieval catacombs, and dwarf warriors, that is to say. All that remained for him was to put together something new and entertaining.

In Markus's game, the building and exploring would occur in a three-dimensional world, which was more inviting and easy to understand than that of Dwarf Fortress.

But, his whole plan changed a couple of days later. Like most evenings after work, Markus was on the computer, when he stumbled upon an indie game he hadn't tried before. It was called Infiniminer. Markus downloaded the game, installed and he started to play, and then almost fell off his chair.

He was stunned by how good the game was - "Oh my God," he thought. "This is genius."

Like Minecraft, Infiniminer involves digging and building. The game was enacted in square, blocky worlds automatically generated before each play. Every individual block can be picked loose from the environment and assembled into something new. Certain blocks, often the ones deep in the ground, contain rare minerals. Others were just dirt and rock to be dug through, in the search for treasure.

The game Infiniminer was developed by American Game developer Zachary Barth and was released in late April 2009, just weeks before Minecraft was released by Markus. The two games' graphics were nearly identical. There are brown dirt blocks, gray stone, and orange, bubbling lava that runs slowly over the ground.

Anyone who played Minecraft, later on, could see that it resembled Infiniminer in a lot of ways.

Infiniminer was originally intended as a multiplayer game, with different teams competing to collect the most precious minerals in the shortest time. Buildings were used as a way of sabotaging the competitors' progress.

But eventually, players discovered that building was more fun than competing for points and they began to spend their time creating houses, castles, and other structures instead.

Infiniminer quickly developed a devoted following, which included Markus, and most signs pointed to Zachary Barth's game being on its way to a breakthrough. But it didn't get there, because of a few unhappy turn of events.

Barely a month after Infiniminer was released, the game's source code was leaked onto the Internet. This meant that anyone with enough programming skills could make changes to the game, and soon, innumerable downloadable copies and variations of Infiniminer began cropping up.

For Zachary Barth, the problem was not material wealth, he had never hoped to make a ton of money from Infiniminer, it was that he lost control of how his game developed. Each of the variations of Infiniminer circulating on the Internet had small, incompatible differences.

Two players with different versions installed could never be sure that they would be able to play with each other. Zachary Barth's plans of building a large and living multiplayer community around Infiniminer became impossible.

Zachary, the American programmer made the best of the situation and released Infiniminer as open source code, and gave his blessing to the game's fans to continue developing it as they wished.

After Markus became familiar with Infiniminer, he immediately sat down and began recoding his own game. He changed the third-person perspective to a first-person point of view and re-did the graphics to make them even more blockish.

It was a step away from the traditional strategy game, he had picked from his old games and towards a more adventure-oriented setup. After a couple of days of frantic coding, Markus leaned back in his chair, satisfied as he saw the puzzle pieces fall into place.

Building, digging and exploring took on a totally new dimension when players saw the world through the eyes of their avatars.

About this time Markus wanted to name his game, So after discussing the matter with some friends at the TIGSource forum, he decided to call his game Minecraft.

The name was a combination of the words mine, for mining ore in shafts, and craft, as in building or creating something. The name was also a wink at Blizzard's strategy games Warcraft and StarCraft, and the enormously successful online role-playing game World of Warcraft.

In early May 2009, Markus uploaded a video recording of a very early version of Minecraft on YouTube. It was a half-finished system for generating worlds and Markus's avatar was gleefully jumping around inside it.

But still, the essence of it hinted at how the game might look when it was done.

In the video Markus said that this was an very early test of an Infiniminer clone he is working on. He said that, it will have more features if he ever get around to finishing it,"

Some might consider what Markus did was a intellectual-property theft, but Markus himself informed everyone, that he found his inspiration from Infiniminer and even went as far as to call Minecraft a clone of Infiniminer.

Markus says game developers, more than other kinds of artists, often find their starting point in an existing idea that they then work on, change, and polish. All studios, large and small, keep tabs on what their competitors were doing and frequently borrow from their games. Game developers seldom accuse others of plagiarizing.

Almost all platform games originated from the mechanics that Nintendo put in place in the first Super Mario Bros., released in 1985. And more or less all role-playing games build on the structure that was developed in games such as The Bard's Tale.

That's why Zachary Barth refused to single out Markus as a thief. He even speaks about how he himself used Team Fortress 2 and the indie game Motherload as inspiration for Infiniminer.

A lot of people asked Zachary if he feels ripped off considering the millions of players and dollars that Minecraft has pulled in.

"The act of borrowing ideas is integral to the creative process. There are games that came before Infiniminer and there are games that will come after Minecraft. That's how it works," said Zachary.

Markus was convinced that he was onto something big, but convincing the world around him of the excellence of his game was not that easy.

Over coffee with his mom, Markus attempted to describe in sweeping gestures the new project he was working on. He told her about the building, the exploration, and the atmosphere, and then explained how the game would be both easily accessible and complicated at the same time. Maybe it could develop into something great, he thought aloud. Maybe he should give notice at work and focus entirely on Minecraft.

Ritva, his mother smiled slightly. She told him that it sounded like a really good idea. In truth, She didn't understand Markus's game idea at all.

She suggested that instead of quitting his job, he can start part-time. She said that It may not be entirely easy to support himself on game development alone.

Secretly, she was worried about her son. she remembered the year after high school, when he didn't look for work, didn't study, and barely went outdoors for days at a time. What would happen if he became just as obsessed with another project, Just like he was obsessed with LEGOs during his elementary school years, which earned him next to nothing.

Even though she was worried, she also noticed how his eyes lit up when he talked about the game. He became confident, self-assured.

At this time, Markus had a girlfriend called Elin Zetterstrand, Elin was a programmer too. When Markus showed her the game, she loved the game.

From that moment on, Elin was Markus's game tester. Every time he added a new feature to Minecraft, he sent her the latest version.

Markus often stood watching over Elin's shoulder while she played, listening intently to her comments. If Elin liked something he had done, he seemed to reason, the rest of the world would probably like it, too.

Even before Minecraft was shown to the public, Markus had made a couple of important decisions that would have a huge influence on the game's continued development.

First, he wanted to document the development openly and in continuous dialogue with players. The players would be from his semiprofessional colleagues at TIGSource and any others who might be interested.

Markus updated his blog often with information about changes in Minecraft and his thoughts about the game's future. He invited everyone who played the game to give him comments and suggestions for improvements.

In addition to that, he released updates often, in accordance with the Swedish saying "hellre än bra" --meaning someone who prefers spontaneity over perfection. As soon as a new function or bug-fix was in place, he made it available via his site, asking players for help in testing and improving it.

Markus knew from the beginning that he eventually wanted people to pay for Minecraft. He was already talking to Jakob, another friend of his who was working at Midasplayer and was discussing their dream of starting their own game studio. So it seemed only natural to put a price on his game.

It sounds normal now to charge for games, but the fact was that Markus's decision went against most of the current trends in the gaming and Internet world.

Many technology experts advocated that to be successful and get lots of money, you should charge as little as possible for your products , preferably nothing at all , attract lots of visitors and put ads on your website.

They pointed to Google and Facebook which gave away products free and earned money through ads.

In the gaming industry, the trend pointed to micropayments. Rovio-developed Angry Birds, which costs one dollar at App Store, and was one of the best-known examples.

Another was the Swedish-developed online game Battlefield Heroes. It was a variation on another popular game that was free to play, but players could buy new equipment and better weapons for a few dollars each.

Markus disregarded all such things. Minecraft was to cost around thirteen dollars during the alpha phase, the first period of development, mainly because it was a sum that he felt comfortable with. When the game was completed, he wanted to double the price.

He says "The reason that I released the game so early, was that I would never have been able to finish it otherwise"

Once he put it out in the world and had made a public commitment, he knew his conscious would keep bothering him.

Charging money was the same thing. He knew that he would never feel that it was good enough to put a price tag on. So he charged from the start, so that it would force him to develop a great game, which users would love.

Markus was notoriously disinterested in business and economics. When someone asked him to reveal the secret behind Minecraft's unbelievable financial success, he just smiles and shrugs his shoulders.

He says, he just followed his gut, did what he felt right and what worked for him. To the question of what was the most important thing he learned from Minecraft's early sales,

Markus says, "I understood that an orange splash where it says 'half price' works really well. That's what I had on the site during the alpha phase."

On May 17, 2009, Markus uploaded the first playable version of Minecraft onto the indie forum TIGSource. "It's an alpha version, so it might crash sometimes," he warned. Other forum writers immediately began exploring the blocky world that Markus presented to them. There was a lot of digging, building, and discussing. The game crashed at times, but even at that early stage, it was clear that Minecraft was exerting an unusual magnetism on players.

Barely an hour after Markus uploaded the game, lots of people commented that they loved the game.

Markus followed the postings with great interest, listening to bug reports and discussing Minecraft's future with others on the forum. He enthusiastically told his friends and family about the warm welcome Minecraft had received.

At that time, every day, many games were uploaded on TIGSource, but few games struck a chord with the audience the way Markus's game did. In his head, a ray of hope began to shine. He thought, maybe he was on the right track this time.

In early June 2009, Markus described his intended pricing model on his blog. Those who paid for the game were promised access to all future updates at no extra cost. A free edition of

Minecraft would still be available, but only the current half-finished version of the game would be available.

For those who bought a copy of Minecraft immediately, there was a discount. When the game entered beta-development, the price would be raised to $20, and the finished version would cost $26. On June 12, 2009, Markus opened his game for orders.

Twenty-four hours later, he checked his sales and could hardly believe his eyes. Fifteen people had paid for the game. In just twenty-four hours, more than $150 had landed in his PayPal account.

This early success encouraged Markus and he obsessively followed the growing sales each day. Seven games purchased per day felt unbelievable for him.

Initially, Markus dismissed these sales as a passing fad. But every day the number of discussion threads about Minecraft on the game developer forum grew larger, and increasing numbers of people visited the forums to read about the game. All the while, the sales kept increasing, slowly at first then faster.

At his home in Sollentuna, Markus did a quick calculation, If he could sell more than twenty games a day, he thought, that would be equal to a decent salary. He made up his mind to quit his day job if he reaches that goal.

Since he was getting some money, he went part-time at his job in order to free himself up to work on his game. He says he had his day job both for security and for preventing him from becoming a total shut-in.

After a year, sales picked up and he finally quit his job on his birthday, June 1st.

Then, he released the full version on the PC, and within twelve months the game got downloaded more than six million times. Markus was struggling to keep up with player requests for new features and bug fixes.

Despite the bold step into full-time indie-game development, he never envisaged Minecraft to become such a widespread success.

He says "I expected it to be about six to twelve months of work, and hoped that it might earn enough money to fund development of a subsequent game."

During this time he had personal problems too. His father relapsed into substance abuse, which he had battled with for years, His drinking was the reason, his marriage to Markus's mother ended earlier.

His father had moved away from Stockholm to avoid the city's influence and also to isolate himself, but he remained interested in and engaged with his son's work. He encouraged his son on his games.

When Markus was deciding whether to quit his day job and work on his own games, his father was the only person who supported Markus's decision. He was proud of Markus and made sure he knew.

PC users were buying 400 copies a day, at about $6 per download. Markus and Jakob quit their day jobs, and Markus even grabbed his old boss, Jalbum CEO Carl Manneh, to run the business side. They named their nascent company Mojang, which means "gadget" in Swedish.

Markus would occasionally visit his father in the Swedish countryside and used to spend time with him.

Markus was planning his father's return to Stockholm and had just rented an apartment for him on the outskirts of the city when his father committed suicide.

He had gotten really drunk and shot himself.

Markus says "It was shocking. It took me a while to even realize it was real."

He didn't break down until he saw his fathers body at the funeral.

At the funeral, everyone asked him, if he wanted some alone time as he hadn't been reacting much. He was calm but when they all left he just crumbled. "I now have an entire life to live without him existing," he thought.

Markus was afraid that if depression has taken over his dad, he may get it too. He knew his father isolated himself from society and moved to a lonely countryside.

Markus not only had lost his father, he began to worry about protecting himself against the demons he had to battle with. "I feel like there is this looming cloud over my life."

Markus knew that the solution was to be in a community and not to isolate himself. That was what he did. He created an alter ego and got a handle called notch and xnotch, to shed his real-world introversion.

He interacted with his players on his blog, twitter and in the TIGSource forum, with his handle.

As the game developed, he got lots more feedback and also requests for an infinite list of potential features to add.

He knew that he can be successful only by being fair to his customers and having a close relationship with them.

He also believed that selling "pre-releases" while developing the game is a great way to both fund development and to gauge how well the things he has added so far works , both technically and in generating money. More sales mean more people are liking it.

He says "We try to make games we want to make for the sake of making fun games and not necessarily to make a profit"

In its first year, Minecraft sold roughly 20,000 downloads. By the end of 2010, it was often selling that many in a day.

Markus got a profit of three million dollars that year and Markus split it among the 25 employees of Mojang.

The community around the game kept growing: Players offered video tutorials suggesting features and pointing out bugs. YouTube channels were devoted to chronicling Minecraft exploits. Forums sprang up discussing the game, players started podcasts, narrating their adventures.

Minecraft was more than a game, it was a platform. Markus became gaming's biggest celebrity.

He amassed 3 million followers on Twitter, where his persona was humorous and brash.

His company Mojang had a flat management structure and loose working hours.

He says ""I don't want to feel like I'm in charge or anything. Of course, it doesn't really work that way, because we all know I'm the founder. But I try to have a studio where people go to make games for the fun of it, not just because some investor has said we have to make money."

Markus and his team were frequently worried, what if the users got bored and stop buying their games. And what if, they would hit a sales slump and not make money.

Markus told them that hopefully, they will keep making money at Mojang, but if they don't, that's fine too. He said they have money to survive for 10 years. They and their employees can just have 10 fun years and at the 10th year, if they don't make money, they can let their employees know, so they can look for new jobs.

In truth, Markus was telling this to console himself and take the pressure off himself.

He says "I think the only way I could make something fun and big is if I don't expect it to be."

Minecraft downloads continued to skyrocket. in 2012, the Xbox 360 version of Minecraft overtook Activision's blockbuster Call of Duty-Modern Warfare as the most played game on the system.

Mojang got bigger and bigger. A lot of big companies like Electronic Arts, Activision and others were interested to buy it. But Markus was hesitant, but finally decided to sell. He ruled out a number of potential buyers and zeroed on one company.

Markus agreed to sell to Microsoft. He made sure that there

will be no layoffs and the founders would not be attached to the company and could leave when desired.

On Sep 15th, 2014, Markus sold his company Mojang to Microsoft for $2.5 billion in cash.

Markus says "Honestly, for something you kind of did by accident, getting $2.5 billion is good enough."

Markus in his blog post said that while Microsoft may technically own Minecraft now "in a much bigger sense, it has belonged to all of you for a long time, and that will never change.".

Markus had a difficult childhood but his passion was gaming. Sometimes he was out of work, but he continued to learn programming for gaming. He loved indie gaming and took an open source game called infiniminer, modified it and created his own game Minecraft. Even though initial sales were low, it picked up and became a huge success. With his single-mother raising him, he rose to build a word famous game and become a billionaire.

When pressed for advice for budding gaming entrepreneurs. He says "Just make games for yourself and try to have a critical eye to what you do,"

"If you genuinely like the game, there will be other people who like it as well."

8
CPK- CALIFORNIA PIZZA KITCHEN

FROM STRESSED-OUT LAWYERS TO MULTIMILLION DOLLAR RESTAURANT ICONS.

Criminal defense lawyers Larry Flax and Rick Rosenfield were in their 40s and getting stressed-out by their full-time jobs.

They quit their jobs as lawyers and started California Pizza Kitchen, which generated millions of dollars in sales.

ॐ

Larry Flax and Rick Rosenfield studied law in college and later on both became federal prosecutors.

They met in 1970 as federal prosecutors, and in 1973, formed their own practice called Flax & Rosenfield.

Larry grew up in Los Angeles, where his dad was doing advertising for the studios. Larry studied law, and in 1968, joined the U.S. Attorney's Office in L.A.

Rick grew up in a family of lawyers in Chicago and ended up in Washington, D.C., working for the Department of Justice. He once visited California on work as a special prosecutor and fell in love. when the opportunity arose, he requested a transfer to Los Angeles.

Both Rick and Larry met in Los Angeles and became good friends.

Larry left his government job in 1971 and opened up his own private practice. He lured Rick to do the same and Rick fell for it and he too left his federal job and joined as a partner.

Both of them traveled extensively in their jobs and were eating at different cities.

That sparked their interest in restaurants plus they always loved to cook. For a short time, they became silent partners in a restaurant. They lost their money on this restaurant, but it whetted their appetites for running a restaurant.

Both of them continued to have dreams of opening a restaurant, but they were getting good money from their lawyer jobs and were not able to quit, dashing their restaurant dreams for a while.

One day a friend said, "You chickenshit lawyers. Are you going to practice law your whole life, or are you going to do what you really want to do?". They told him they were not ready yet, but secretly they were afraid to jump full in.

That was in 1984. At that time, they were commuting to San Francisco for 2½ months on a currency-fraud trial. By then, Rick got married and his wife had a baby, and Larry had a girlfriend in Houston. Their lawyer work was lucrative, but they were getting burned out with traveling.

They had been thinking of leaving the law practice for a while now but their fear did not allow them to move forward. The case they were handling in San Francisco was so frustrating. They thought the facts were in their favor, but they got a hung jury. That broke the camel's back. They came back to L.A. and said, "Let's go into the restaurant business."

Both of them did not know anything about the restaurant business. First, they finalized a place for their restaurant and then they moved their law office next to it too. They didn't want to quit their jobs at the beginning stages. They wanted to work on their Jobs and on their restaurant.

As days passed, it was getting difficult to work on both the restaurant and the lawyer job.

So Rick stopped practicing six months before opening and focused full time on the restaurant, While Larry kept the practice going and supported Rick financially.

They were not sure, what type of restaurant to start.

One time, they were in Chicago and saw a pasta restaurant. So, they decided to start a pasta business. They decided to check out a similar pasta restaurant in Glendale, California.

When they went there, they noticed that a not-particularly-good pizza going around and even though the pizza was not good, half of the people were having a slice.

That day they decided to go with a pizza restaurant and not with the pasta restaurant, they had thought of earlier.

Next, the two friends needed a concept for their restaurants. They looked around for other successful pizza restaurants for inspiration.

They found it in the kitchens of two other LA-Area chefs, Alice Waters of Chez Panisse restaurant and Wolfgang Puck of Spago restaurant.

These chefs were making high-end pizzas, using ingredients such as smoked salmon, duck sausage and goat cheese.

Legendary chef Wolfgang Puck introduced "California-style pizza," topped with ingredients that had never before been seen atop a pizza, like smoked salmon, caviar, zucchini blossoms, and flavored olive oils.

And while these were inventive and flavorful pizzas, Rick and Larry realized that they weren't accessible to most Americans because they were very expensive.

Larry says " What we were really doing was emulating Spago and Wolfgang Puck-style wood-burning-oven pizza and bringing it to the masses, taking it from high-end, reservation-only restaurants to a more accessible restaurant".

To open the restaurant they needed half a million dollars. They took out second mortgages on their houses and drained their savings and pooled a total of $250,000. They still needed another $250,000.

They had no idea what they were doing but signed a lease in Beverly Hills. They still needed more money and they thought of borrowing the rest.

But when they asked investors, everyone was very skeptical. "Two lawyers going into the pizza business? That's crazy," they said. They were not getting any money.

When they approached banks, they turned them down immediately. "The bankers were mortified," says Rick.

Then they called 23 of their family and friends, they got 22 yeses, and raised $300,000.

They made all their investors as limited partners in the company.

They wondered how they could compete against experienced restaurant owners.

They found a simple answer and that was to learn from those with prior experience.

Larry and Rick began by turning to one of the most successful restaurateurs in history, Ray Kroc, the founder of McDonald's.

Rick says "If you go back, the first one we looked to and read everything about was Ray Kroc.

There was a book called "Behind the Golden Arches," and then Ray Kroc himself had an autobiography, so we sort of read those things cover to cover a lot of times."

They wrote a very unsophisticated business plan. It basically said they were going to create the third style of pizza, New York, Chicago, and now California. That was pretty bold for two guys who hadn't been in the restaurant business.

So, on March 27, 1985, they opened their first California Pizza Kitchen in Beverly Hills, California.

They relocated their law practice next to their first restaurant site, with the idea that they would open the restaurant and maintain the law practice too. But when clients came to know that these lawyers opened a pizza restaurant, no new customers hired them. "We never got a new legal client," says Larry.

Opening night was crazy bad. Someone made a reservation for 7:30 p.m. for his son's 16th birthday party and was late. The place was jammed and Larry and Rick had to deal with angry people waiting in line, while there was an empty table for twelve in the middle of the restaurant. The next night, they stopped taking reservations.

The california-style pizza was just emerging. When Wolfgang Puck's high-end Spago restaurant opened, people couldn't get in for weeks as they were booked for several weeks. The pizzas were very expensive and the restaurant mostly catered to the wealthy.

Rick's and Larry's idea was to bring Spago style restaurant to the masses. They talked to Ed LaDou, the cook from Spago and he agreed to consult for them. Ed, the cook created the original CPK menu, with things like rabbit sausage, radicchio, pine nut, grape-leaf pizza.

They introduced this menu in their restaurant and to their utter disbelief, none of these pizzas sold. But, what did sell, was the barbecue chicken pizza and this was also created by Ed.

Rick says "That's where the future was, taking items people loved and putting it on pizza. So Larry and I created a new menu. "

Their next success was the Thai chicken pizza. Customers loved their Pizza's and revenue slowly started to trickle in.

It was clear that they were not going to make enough money from one restaurant to make a living. They decided to open a second restaurant but did not have enough money.

Since their first restaurant was a little successful, they approached the previous family and friends and converted them from limited partners to shareholders. They then told them that they can put money into the company.

A lot of their investors were people they had invited for tastings in their first restaurant. These investors could see that they had a location and they knew what the menu was going to be. So, they believed the second restaurant would succeed too.

So they invested in their second restaurant too. Every time they needed money, they sent a letter to their shareholder base and most of them would invest again.

By the end of the first year, they did close to $1.5 million in revenue, which they had never expected.

As lawyers, they were cautious and logical. Larry says "If we had known then what we know now, we would never have opened a restaurant. Sometimes you have to be blind to risk and just take it. Once you take the first step, you just keep going."

By 1992, they had grown to 25 restaurants and $50+ million in revenues.

Both the founders felt that they should guard their reputation. Larry says "You can have a full house, but if you don't serve people quickly enough, they get mad and word spreads."

They also noticed that people wanted to stay a little bit after they eat their meal.

So, they created an environment where diners can relax and stick around after finishing their slices.

When they wanted to create branding, they took inspiration from Starbucks logo.

Larry says "I've often said I want to own yellow like Starbucks owns green,"

"The Starbucks logo, if you asked somebody to describe it, most people can't tell you what it really is." "By the way, it is a mermaid."

Larry adds "But you sure know it, when you see it, you recognize that green, and you don't have to read much about it. So we decided that's really an important part of the logo."

CPK made its sunny yellow color more prominent in its logo to create a stronger brand-color association in customers' minds.

For nickname ideas, the co-founders looked to Col. Sanders, the founder of KFC, Kentucky fried chicken.

Larry says "When we were doing our logo, it didn't escape us that Kentucky Fried Chicken was KFC". "So there was something about our letters that worked in our mind. And now, little kids call it CPK. We've given little kids an easy way to identify with us."

In 1991, They were brainstorming where to put the smoking and nonsmoking sections.

For some reason, they did not like people smoking in their restaurants. They decided to remove the smoking section completely. CPK became the first national restaurant chain to go non-smoking.

With an upscale menu of creative pizzas, pastas, and salads, it slowly developed legions of fans.

Each location had nearly 20 varieties of cheeses on hand. They also continued to introduce new menu items. They introduced new summer items in June and winter items in November. Occasionally, they also took off items that did not sell well.

Asked how they come up with new ideas for the menu, Rick says, sometimes he looks at another restaurant, sometimes a food type that is popular. When they first started, Thai food was popular and everybody was rushing to Thai restaurants and dipping everything they eat in peanut satay sauce.

He thought, the sauce was an adult way of eating peanut butter, adults getting a peanut butter fix. So he created the Thai Chicken Pizza with satay on it and it became a hit.

He had many menu failures too. In 1987, when they were opening the Brentwood restaurant, he came up with an egg salad pizza. Unfortunately, It was the same week the government came out with a report, that eggs were very high in cholesterol. The menu didn't do well, and they took it off the menu quickly.

Since Larry loves cooking, his wife built a big giant kitchen for him at their house. "I do like to cook and play with different ideas at home," he says.

When they are home, Larry does the cooking. "To me, cooking is an art form," he says. His wife Joan, cooks on holidays.

Larry says "My hobby is my work. If you love what you do, you'll never work a day in your life – that's an old Confucius saying. That's true, so, therefore, you don't need hobbies when you love what you do. "

When they wanted to expand to frozen foods and Mini restaurants in malls and airports, they studied Baskin-Robbins. They studied Baskin-Robbins' growth and some of the problems they had.

For instance, when they went into all of their franchise agreements, like with the Mirage Hotel, they always made sure they had the right to go into the frozen food case.

Larry says "Baskin-Robbins made the mistake of expanding and franchising before deciding to go into the frozen food case. They were sort of locked out by their franchisee agreements.

That's what gave Haagen-Dazs, the foothold to come in and really grow through the frozen food case."

From a single store in Beverly Hills in 1985, the company expanded to more than 250 locations in more than 30 states and 11 countries including Japan and Hong Kong., drawing in revenue of more than US$500 million.

CPK slowly became the uncontested leader in the California-style pizza marketplace.

Knowing and reading about other companies' trials, successes and failures helped them tremendously. They flat-out avoided mistakes.

They also skipped trial-and-error because they knew what worked and did not work for other similar chains.

Anyone could get a plain pepperoni slice, but the restaurant's signature BBQ Chicken pizza crust topped with barbecue sauce, smoked Gouda, red onions and cilantro, is what put California Pizza Kitchen on the culinary map.

Today, diners can order pizzas in off-the-beaten-path varieties such as Thai Chicken, Wild Mushroom and California Club, which comes topped with avocado, arugula, basil, and romaine that has been tossed in a lemon-pepper salad dressing.

It was tough for the friends to stay together when disagreements arose between them.

Larry says "Over the years it was our synergy that pulled us through. We never walked away mad from disagreements. We always argued like lawyers and brought the other one around."

Rick says "When people talk about it being lonely at the top, we never had that. We shared the decisions. We both have healthy egos, but we were never vested in being right. That's one of the great secrets to our success."

CPK was growing well and many companies wanted to buy them. Larry and Rick were hesitant.

After thinking a lot, finally, In 2011, the pair sold CPK to San Francisco private investment firm Golden Gate Capital for about $470 million.

Rick says "Be well-capitalized. So many concepts fail because the entrepreneurs misjudge how long it takes them to be successful."

Larry adds "Be optimistic. Bad times create an opening of doors. A lot of people might think this is a terrible time, but it's not. There is a lot of money out there for good ideas. These are times when optimists can really take advantage. Now is the time to strike."

After they opened their first restaurant in 1985, it was very successful and they did not return back to law practice ever. When asked if they miss the law practice, they said "Never".

Two friends Larry and Rick started out as lawyers but were

stressed out by their jobs. They found out that their passion was in Restaurants. Even though they did not know anything about opening restaurants, they learned from other successful entrepreneurs and kept moving.

They struggled initially and faced many problems, but they came out successfully and built a multi-million dollar restaurant empire.

Larry says "We had learned a lot. We had opened up a ton of restaurants and made mistakes. The mistakes become lessons."

"Every step of the way, we believed in the concept." "In entrepreneurship, that keeps you rolling," adds Larry.

9
CRAIGSLIST

A POVERTY-STRICKEN POOR BOY TO A MULTI-MILLIONAIRE INTERNET ICON

Sometimes, amazing businesses are built by a driven founder obsessed with a single idea. But then there's Craigslist.

This ragtag online classified website happened by accident, had a very bad design as per the experts, and has always been run by individuals apparently allergic to virtually every deeply held beliefs of business and management.

They never went after money, never went after crazy growth. It nonetheless became one of the lasting icons of the internet and is, by all reckonings, insanely profitable and is estimated to be worth more than a billion dollars.

The man behind it, is the remarkable entrepreneur and do-gooder in this universe, Craig Newmark.

❧

Craig Alexander Newmark was born on December 6, 1952, in Morristown, New Jersey, to Joyce and Lee Newmark. Lee, Craig's father worked as a salesman who peddled everything from food to insurance. Life was a little tough for the family with limited money.

As fate would have it, Craig's father died of lung cancer shortly after his 13th birthday. His mother Joyce had to move her two sons, Craig and Jeff into a less expensive apartment.

Craig used to frequent the junkyard close to his home and grew up in poverty.

His mother worked as a bookkeeper and struggled to make ends meet after her husband passed away. Craig went to Morristown High School, where he became co-captain of the debate team, and also an active member of the forensics club. He also started his own club, which met regularly to play the game Go.

In his third grade, his dream was to become a paleontologist, a scientist who studies fossils.

When he moved to high school, he was a full-on nerd. He used to wear thick black glasses taped together and taped his torn shirt pocket with a pocket protector. Other kids did not want to be friends with him and he was lonely.

He says he never realized that these things made him unattractive.

His definition of nerd has to do with a lack of social instinct for people, a lack of learned and ingrained social skills. He says he was reasonably socialized for some time, but around the fifth or sixth grade, his social skills didn't develop. he didn't gain the normal instincts people had for how to relate to others. "I have since learned social skills and I can simulate them for short periods, but I do feel somewhat detached," he says.

After graduating from Morristown High School in 1971, Craig had earned enough scholarships to fund his post-secondary education at Case Western Reserve University. There, he received a Bachelor of Science degree in 1975 and a Masters of Science degree in 1977.

It was at Case Western University, where he got a first glimpse of Arpanet, the precursor to the internet. In this early days, Arpanet was basically used only by the scientist community.

He never realized its potential back then and did not show interest, He was too focused on class work.

With his new degrees, Craig landed himself, a job as a programmer with IBM. For the next 17 years, he worked at IBM, first in Boca Raton, Florida and then in Detroit. At IBM, he learned that his lack of social skills held him back professionally too.

In 1984, he read a book called Neuromancer, by William Gibson. He saw the vision of what cyberspace could be. He also understood that regular people, having no power or influence, could work together to accumulate power from the grassroots up.

At that time, Craig realized that this vision had kicked off the imaginations of many other people and it did for Craig too.

in the early '90s, he started seeing that vision again in the internet community. So, he started spending time on the WELL, a small but highly influential virtual community on the internet.

In 1993, after 17 years working at IBM, he left IBM and joined Charles Schwab and moved to San Francisco. At Schwab they had a brown-bag-luncheon series where he would go around the company evangelizing the Internet, telling people how the equity brokerage business would work someday with the internet. Not a lot of people knew about the internet at that time.

Unfortunately, he got laid off from Charles Schwab in 1995. He then started looking for work

and began working as a contract programmer, taking on contracts with Bank of America, Sun Microsystems and others.

Craig was always interested in helping out people. On the internet, he saw a lot of people helping other people out using the internet and he figured, that he should do something too to help out other people.

In his first year or two in San Francisco, a lot of people helped him acclimatize to this new town. They helped him understand what neighborhoods were good, where to shop etc. He got a lot out of it. So, he decided he should give back.

So, on March 1, 1995, he started emailing out notices about cool events, what he thought were cool events to friends. He sent it to around 10 to 12 people using a text-based email software called Pine. These were usually arts and technology events. Craig was 42 years of age at this time.

He started with two events: The first was Joe's Digital Diner, where people would come and display the use of multimedia technology. Multimedia was just emerging then. Around a dozen people would come and have dinner, mostly spaghetti and meatballs, around a big table.

The second event was a party called the Anon Salon, which was very theatrical but also technology focused.

His friends started liking these emails about the cool events and told their friends. Then more people kept emailing him, requesting for their email addresses to be added to Craig's email list.

More people wanted to be added to the list. They just kept emailing him asking for their addresses to be added to his email list.

Everyone who received the emails were calling it as "Craig's List."

As time went by, Craig just kept listening to his users. At first, his email was just about arts and technology events. Then some subscribers asked him, if he could pass on a post about a job or something for sale to his email list.

Craig could sense an apartment shortage growing, so he asked his subscribers to send apartment needed ads.

This lead to the addition of a category for "apartments", Then he added a category for "jobs". Slowly, additional categories were added in response to user demand.

As tasks started getting difficult, Craig would usually write some code to automate these tasks.

In the middle of 1995, his subscribers swelled and the Pine email software he was using, to send emails couldn't handle his bigger CC list.

The email list had reached over 240 subscribers, and he could no longer send his emails in one batch; even his cc field on his email client would not accept any more email addresses.

So, he decided to use a listserv named Majordomo. The listserv was designed to send emails to a group of people. He also wanted to give it a formal name.

He was going to call it "SFEvents" for San Francisco Events, but his friends and readers, who were calling it craigslist advised him to keep calling it with the same name. They told him that, it feels personal and quirky.

Craig agreed with them and kept the Craigslist name. He says that is how Craigslist always evolved. People would suggest things to him, and then he would figure out what seemed to make sense, what a lot of people were asking for, and then he would do it.

Sometime in late '95, he realized that he had many folders on his computer for different categories like jobs, apartment listings, buy/ sell items etc. Craigslist had expanded into more categories and he was keeping these lists in many different folders.

He realized that instead of emailing the list, maybe he should create a website.

Also, by this time, it was growing in popularity and his community members requested a web interface too.

Craig was good at coding, particularly in a programming language called Perl.

To create a website, he sat down and coded a program which

could turn all these text lists in these different folders into web pages.

Then, he registered the website called Craigslist.org and he put up the website with the lists he had.

The response was slow. He says their traffic has always been slow but grows slowly. Craig says "We're the tortoise, not the hare. Now and then we'll get a surge of growth, but it's been slow but steady."

At this time, he was still working on his day job and doing Craigslist on the side.

When he was working on his contract programming job, he worked out an arrangement with the people that he was working for that he would be working on his side hustle Craigslist a little bit here and there.

Now and then, he would look at his craigslist email and used to get some of his stuff done. Sometimes, he would put in a half hour doing his contracting work, then he would take a half hour off to do craigslist, and then he would get back to work.

He ran the entire craigslist operations from his apartment. Craigslist continued to grow. By the end of 1997, the website was getting about one million page views a month which was big at that time.

Even though it had high traffic numbers and growth, he was the only person working on the website. At that point, the PR people from Microsoft Sidewalk approached him about running banner ads.

He was in a dilemma whether to run banner ads on his website or not. He was not much interested in making money. After much deliberations, he decided not to do them, because they would slow the site down and he also thought they were kind of dumb.

They would not be relevant to his users but would only distract them. He says Banner ads are, more often than not, kind of dumb.

More importantly, he thought about his own values and thought about how much money, does he need.

He was already doing well as a contractor. So he figured that the money from his contracting job was enough for him and he would not put the banner ads just to make money. So, he declined to put banner ads.

He says "At that point, I got the first inkling of what I now call my "moral compass.".

He saw many people out there who were claiming they hold their morals high but actually didn't practice what they preached.

"It's about time for people of goodwill to reassert their idea of what's right and what's wrong, " he says.

Once he decided that the site was good the way it was and he didn't need any more money, he stuck to that but expanded on it later on.

Around the end of 1998, they took a good look at the morality of charging for something. They asked a lot of craigslist users for advice. They also asked them, if they should charge for every category or for specific categories.

Most of the people in the craigslist community they talked to, said they should not charge for everything but can charge for Job ads and charge landlords and apartment brokers.

They stuck with that. The Craigslist community primarily dictated the policy and they weren't shy about sending the feedback in.

So, they started charging $25 for job postings in San Francisco ads to cover website costs.

At the end of 1997, he was approached by some volunteers, who suggested to run craigslist as a nonprofit and see. Craig thought it was a good idea and went ahead and tried running it as a non-profit.

The idea was that, instead of employees, volunteers would help the website.

Craig thought it was a good idea and made the changes to the company to be run as a non-profit.

But things did not work out well. The listings were not getting posted on time, the database didn't get pruned of old listings in a consistent way and many other issues were cropping up.

Craig realized that he would not be able to run his website as a non-profit.

"To make a long, painful story short, that effort failed. I kind of knew it was failing, probably midway through 1998, but I was in denial. " Craig says.

At this time, a couple of his biggest job posters took Craig out for lunch and told him that running Craigslist as a non-profit wasn't working. They told him to get real and run craigslist as a serious business.

He also realized that there were a lot of legal constraints in nonprofits and they are meant to prevent various forms of corruption.

It took Craig a couple of months, but he got out of denial and changed craigslist into a for-profit company.

So in 1999, he incorporated the company and started hiring full-time people in all the areas they needed, including billing, customer service, and technology.

At this time, he was working as a Java programmer for a startup called Continuity Solutions, which was building customer service software. He was still working part-time on Craigslist, but it came with extra perks. Because of Craigslist, he got invitations to attend the best parties for geeks and nerds out there.

Till this time, Craig was running it more like a hobby, but now Craig decided that he has to get real and decided to commit himself to the business.

So he quit his job and came in full time to work on Craigslist. "I left it because I had to get serious about craigslist, " he says.

Even though he quit, he knew that the money from Craigslist was not sufficient for his living expenses.

Craig says, in the conventional sense, they were never a startup. A startup is a company, with a great idea, that becomes a serious corporation. Startups usually have a business plan and strategy and bring in serious investment, and they want to make a lot of money.

But at Craigslist, they did something very different. They stepped away from a huge amount of money and did not take outside funding and never really had a strategy.

Craig says "in our case, we built something, we get feedback, we try to figure out what makes sense out of these suggestions, and then we do something about it and then we listen some more."

Craigslist success came about through a series of small steps and adjusting as they went and not through any huge pre-defined strategy.

From the very beginning, they had the blessing of very limited resources, which meant they couldn't do fancy stuff. So instead, they just progressed in small increments.

Craig says "We progress a little on the slow side, which may mean we lose some opportunity. But we respond to real needs and try to do really well, in terms of helping out people and that seems to work."

Craig adds "We're innovative in many small ways. When we see something that could be done better, we do it. This is the notion of kaizen, the Japanese practice of continuous business process re-engineering."

Craig used to talk to a lot of bankers and VC's socially but was never interested in their money. These Bankers and VC's were beginning to fantasize about the way the internet could happen. They were telling him to do the normal Silicon Valley thing of trying to make more money from his website.

They were saying that Craigslist could be a billion-dollar

company. But Craig had already made the decision to not highly monetize when he first turned down the banner ads offer from Microsoft.

For a while, he was running craigslist out of his apartment, Later he hosted it with a hosting service provider. He was always worried that if they have an issue with the service in the middle of the night, he may not be able to reach this service provider.

The year when he started craigslist, he knew that he was not good at managing people."People helped me understand that, as a manager, I kind of sucked." he says.

He had trouble making tough decisions. He was not good at the job interview process and he made mistakes. He found it very difficult to fire anyone. He couldn't make major decisions that required some boldness, like adding new cities. He knew that he needed to expand to more cities "but I guess I didn't have the guts to do it." he says.

He thought that maybe they needed to do some advertising in an HR magazine, for job postings

in those new cities.

So he hired someone to do marketing and put up a couple of ads, and he realized that, this was just a wasted effort and that word of mouth was what really worked.

But he made one really good hiring decision, which was choosing their CEO, Jim Buckmaster. He saw his résumé at the end of 1999 and hired him around then, as a lead tech guy. Craig later realized that Jim could run things better than he could.

After he hired Jim, Craig was still CEO and he learned to keep his ego aside from his CEO role and took in the advise given by Jim to improve the operations of Craigslist.

He had seen micromanagement as a big problem in the tech industry and he decided not to do this with Jim. "I just saw lots of situations where people screwed up by interfering with people who could do the job," he says.

Jim contributed to the site's multi-city architecture, its search engine, discussion forums, flagging system, self-posting process, homepage design, personals categories and also the "best-of-Craigslist" feature.

Craig knew that Jim would be a better CEO than him. So, in November of 2000 Craig promoted Jim as CEO. Craig stepped down as CEO and moved to the customer service department.

With characteristic modesty, Craig continued to refer himself not as a founder but as a "customer service representative."

By April of 2000, there were nine Craigslist employees working out of Craig's San Francisco apartment, including Jim Buckmaster.

Craigslist continued to grow. By 2004, it was earning over $10 million in revenues.

Craig says "What seems to make craigslist work is our deal about "doing well by doing good," and by providing a platform where people can help others with everyday basic stuff. That starts with helping get a job and a home, and goes from there."

When he started the website, he did not worry much about spammers and other people trying to take advantage of his site to spam.

They had a really good culture of trust on the site. They found that pretty much everyone out there shared the same moral compass as they do. Craig says "People are good. There are some bad guys out there, but they are a very tiny minority "

He says what surprises him, was how almost universally people are trustworthy and good. "No matter what your religious background, we share pretty much the same values," he says.

He adds that there are problems, and sometimes people bicker, which is a pain in the ass, but people are good.

Their community was self-policing. He says that people wanted other people to play fair.

He set up a way for the community to regulate the site and introduced flagging. If someone sees someone posting bad stuff, they would flag him. If many people flag it, Craig and his team would know about it and will remove that posting.

By virtue of flagging, they turned over control of their site, for the most part, on a day-to-day basis to the people who use the site.

But still, spammers attacked them. But they kept plugging the holes, fixed the issues and kept moving ahead.

Although it started as a side project, Craig was always very committed from the beginning.

"I'm stubborn. As I sometimes say, "I'm one very persistent nerd." he says.

When he joined craigslist full time, since he didn't make money initially, he had to live on his savings

for several months. Luckily he had saved up some money and he kept his expenses low and managed his website.

He funded it with his own time and money initially. He never took any investment. When he was trying to run Craigslist as a non-profit, he took a small loan in the low thousands.

Most of the time, users would give them feedback and ask for features. They would then build these features.

Asked if he had any grand vision for Craigslist when he started, he says, he had nothing in mind other than telling people about arts and technology events in San Francisco and pretty much everything on the site was based on user feedback.

"Frankly, I have no vision whatsoever.," says Craig.

Slowly, people got really attached to the website. Communities began to form out of classified ads and events listings.
"We're not certain how it happened, except that we really do listen to people. We try to treat people like we want to be treated, and somehow we built a culture of trust. " Craig says.

Asked if there are any similarities between Wikipedia and Craigslist, he says that both sites are built by the people who use them. Both have a culture of trust, and both are part of an historic trend where power is flowing from small groups of powerful people to much larger, but still small, groups of people.

He adds that both sites, like a lot of others, suffer from the same problem of being attacked by disinformation professionals and that's an ongoing problem everywhere else on the internet too.

Craigslist continued to grow and by 2010, it was generating more than $122 million annually.

Asked why he has not changed the design to a fanciful design, he admits that he doesn't know how to design fancy.

The evolution of Craigslist was based on listening to people as to what they wanted and what was needed. People consistently told them that they didn't want fancy stuff; they wanted something simple, straightforward, and fast. So, they listened to consensus rather than what someone was trying to talk them into.

Sometimes they may hear, from 10 people who love the fancy stuff, and who would say, that they should change the design to a fancy design, and then they would hear from a million other people asking them to keep the site design simple. So they stuck with simple because the majority of them wanted it to keep it simple.

Slowly they started to charge for apartment rental listings in New York City and the site was starting to make money. They were still charging for less than 1 percent of the site. In fact, the apartment brokers asked him to charge them, because they felt that it will help improve the quality of the listings shown on the website and it will also help control the sleazier brokers.

But even then, some brokers tried to do bad things. One time, a broker tried to post using multiple email addresses. Craig just kept blocking them and blocking them, and they finally got tired of being blocked and they finally approached him and told him that they made a mistake and after this, they behaved fine and posted according to craigslist guidelines.

Investors looked at the growth and wanted to invest. Craig was tempted to go for it, but he decided to hold fast. He says there is nothing wrong in getting investments and he is not anti-traditional by any means. It was just that, they made a decision not to get investments based on their specific values and followed through.

Lots of companies wanted to buy Craigslist and approached them. They firmly said no.

But hell broke loose. One of the employee who got some stock grant left the company and sold his equity to eBay. eBay bought a 28.4 percent stake in Craigslist in 2004.

Craig was a little upset. "What it taught me is that partners of any sort need to be trustworthy," he says.

Years ago, in his earlier days, Craig decided to grant stock options, because he thought that would help him avoid the temptation to sell his company if he has sole control over it. He never expected his employees to sell it to anyone.

Luckily for Craig, eBay had a similar moral compass as craigslist and they never interfered with what craigslist was doing.

While working in those big organizations like IBM and Charles Schwab, he saw that people formed factions or silos and operated on their own, sometimes detached from the company's purpose.

"We are very different from any other startup you've heard about," Craig says.

Craig deliberately decided not to grow very big. He wanted to shape the culture of his company and so he wanted to keep his employee count low and never wanted to grow too big and have too many employees.

They also did not spend a lot of money for the office space. Oddly enough, they moved into an old Victorian mansion in a not-great location in San Francisco.

To find employees, they used to advertise on craigslist itself.

He says that the most important part of their company culture is trust. Craig calls it "The moral compass".

Craig says people sometimes still think that they are a nonprofit, even though they tell people that they are not. He adds that sometimes people think that they sold part of craigslist to eBay, and "that's a misconception, I have to fix now and then" he adds.

When starting a startup, "Trust your instincts and your moral compass" Craig says.

To Craig, Craigslist is about having a business that helps people help each other out.

Craig says more than anything else, the timing is what mattered in the success of craigslist.

But when he built Craigslist, he was building something that people really wanted and there wasn't anything like that out there.

When he started it, all he thought was giving a little bit back to the community.

"It was just a little hobby and the only difference between a little hobby and what we have now is that we follow through, " he says.

In the Bay Area, Craigslist has fast become a local institution, and Craig Newmark himself, much to his bashful chagrin, has become at once, an urban legend and a local celebrity. Some people don't believe that there is a real guy named Craig, and they express incredulity when meeting him in person.

Others seek him out to tell him, how Craigslist has changed their lives, how a roommate became a spouse, or how a gig jump-started a career. "That feels pretty good," Craig says with characteristic understatement.

In December 2012, Craig married Eileen Whelpley in New Jersey. Craig had been dating Whelpley for about a year after meeting each other on Cole Street in San Francisco. They both settled together in San Francisco.

Craig does a lot of non-profit work with his organization Craig connects and sits on the board of several other organizations like the Center for Public Integrity and the Sunlight Foundation.

Craigslist is now in 700 cities in 70-plus countries and remains one of the most-trafficked sites in the U.S.

Even though Craigslist is free for almost everybody, it still makes more than $120 million annually.

Its main source of revenue is still primarily from the paid job ads in select cities. It charges $75 per ad in San Francisco and $25 per ad in New York, Los Angeles and now San Diego, Boston, Seattle, Washington, D.C., Chicago, Philadelphia, Orange County in California, and Portland, Oregon. It also charges $10 per paid broker apartment listing ad in New York City.

Despite being one of the biggest websites in the world, the company still has only about 40 employees.

Things changed with eBay too. In 2015, Craigslist finally settled with eBay and bought back the remaining shares and took full control.

Now more than 50 million people visit Craigslist each month. The website gets over 20 billion page views, 80 million new classified advertisements, and 2 million new job posting listings each month, making it the leading classifieds service and one of the top job boards in the world.

"The stuff that works best, is driven by passion rather than dollars," Craig says.

Yet, Craig became a multi-millionaire. Forbes conservatively estimates that Craigslist is worth at least $3 billion.

Craig Newmark's life is very interesting and different from many entrepreneurs.

He grew up in poverty after his father died unexpectedly. He never had grand plans for his life.

At the age of 42, he wanted to give back and help people. He started an email list and sent his friends the interesting tech events in San Francisco.

Even for craigslist, he did not have any business plan or grand vision. He just had the goal of helping people and he took feedback from friends and his users and grew Craigslist very slowly.

By every sense, he did not follow the regular startup success principles and he should have failed. Yet this poor and humble kid surprised everyone and built Craigslist as one of the iconic brands on the internet and became a multi-millionaire.

Craig says "There's no genius behind it. It's persistence and listening to people." "I regard my life over the past 20 years as completely surreal."

He adds "I never thought my hobby would become a successful business".

But it did, and it made him a legend.

10
HERSHEY'S CHOCOLATES

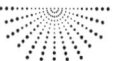

A POOR FOURTH GRADE DROPOUT TO A WORLD-FAMOUS BILLIONAIRE CHOCOLATIER

The founder of Hershey's Chocolates, Milton Hershey, had many failures in business.

His path to sweet success was fraught with obstacles and setbacks that would have crushed lesser men. But through perseverance, ingenuity and his amazing ability to bounce back from failure, he built one of America's great fortunes from the ground up and brought joy to millions and in doing so, he immortalized his name, Hershey's Chocolates.

He just had a fourth-grade education and he learned everything as he went along.

Milton Hershey was born on September 13, 1857, in Derry Township, Pennsylvania. He had a sister named Serina.

His mother, Fanny, was a devoted Mennonite. His father, Henry, was a dreamer who always had his eye out for the next big opportunity. But Henry Hershey, his father lacked the perseverance and work ethic to stick to any one thing.

He would start something and if it failed, he would move on to the next one. He never stuck to one thing.

When Milton was nine years old, his sister died from Scarlet fever. Milton was devastated. It took some time for him to come out of this sadness.

Because his dad moved them around a lot. Milton Hershey did not have much education.

His parents eventually separated and his father moved to Denver.

By 1867, Hershey's father had largely cut himself out of the family picture. The details around his parents' separation are not clear, but it's largely believed that it was caused by his father's many failures.

With Milton's upbringing left to her, the strict Fanny instilled in her son an appreciation for hard work. While he was in 4th grade, his mother decided that Milton should leave school and learn a trade.

Milton's mother found him an apprentice job with a newspaper printer. He would help, set up each letter for the printing press and then load the paper and ink for the printer to work. He found the work to be boring and didn't enjoy the job.

He decided that printing was not the right profession for him. so he started to look for something which he would like.

So, at the age of 14, Milton, who'd dropped out of school the year before, expressed an interest in candy making. He began apprenticing with Joseph Royer, a master confectioner in Lancaster, Pennsylvania from the Lancaster confectionery shop.

He learned a great deal from Royer and he blossomed under Royer's tutelage, acquiring many of the skills and tools he would later use to build his own empire.

Milton learned the art of candy making. He made all sorts of candy including caramels, fudge, and peppermints. He really enjoyed being a candy maker and knew he had found what he wanted to do for the rest of his life.

Four years later, at the age of 19, he decided to open his own candy business. The problem is, he did not have enough money.

He convinced his aunt Mattie and borrowed $150 from her and set up his own candy shop in the heart of Philadelphia.

For five long years, Hershey poured his sweat and time into the business.

He worked day and night to keep his business alive. Working 15 to 16 hours a day and sleeping only for 4-5hours a day, Hershey would make caramels and taffies at night, then sell them from a pushcart to crowds at the Great Centennial Exposition, which was being held to celebrate the 100th anniversary of the Declaration of Independence.

He was working so hard and one day, due to sheer exhaustion, he collapsed. He recovered slowly and immediately started to work again.

Unfortunately, no matter how hard Milton worked, he couldn't figure out how to get his business to make a profit.

So in February 1882, after a winter dogged by illness and mounting debt, Hershey had to close down his business. But, deep down in his heart, he still knew candy making was his passion.

He headed to Denver and joined his father in the great Colorado silver rush.

He got a job as a confectioner in Denver and he learned that adding fresh milk to caramel greatly improved its quality and extended the candy's shelf life, a discovery that would be crucial in later years.

He also found that the milk made the caramels creamier and chewier too. But the entrepreneur in Milton wasn't content to work for someone else, and he struck out on his own again.

He moved to Chicago and opened another candy business. But this too failed!. He couldn't make it work.

He moved to New York and undeterred, he opened another candy business.

In New York, one day while he was making a sales call at a candy store, he saw a beautiful girl and fell in love instantly.

Her name was Catherine Sweeney, and her nickname was "Kitty," and she hailed from Jamestown, New York. Milton and Catherine continued to meet often.

Despite his best efforts, his business continually lost money. When a group of kids stampeded his delivery wagon and made off with his entire stock, Hershey was bankrupt.

He failed again this time too.

Success still eluded him, but Milton had a dogged persistence. He was determined to find a way.

In 1883, he returned to Lancaster, Pennsylvania his home state and he was still convinced he could build a successful candy company.

He wanted to open another business, but no one wanted to lend him money as he had too many failures.

His relatives had given up on him, refusing even to take him in, let alone lend him money to start another business.

But Hershey would soon find salvation in the form of an old friend and employee.

Henry Lebkicher, who had briefly worked for Hershey in his Philadelphia store, not only offered Hershey a place to live but also lent him the money he needed to bring his candy-making equipment from New York.

The pair then scraped together enough capital to start the business that would firmly establish Milton Hershey as a candy-maker. He started the Lancaster Caramel Co.

He then experimented with all sorts of different candies and chocolates. The area where he lived had lots and lots of dairy farms, so he had a large and easy supply of fresh milk.

Drawing from his experiences in Denver, Hershey began experimenting with using fresh milk in the candy-making process.

Despite his failures, he managed to create a recipe for

caramels that used fresh milk, making it much creamier than the hard ones they used to get at that time.

He called his unique confection "Hershey's Crystal A" caramels.

This new recipe was a success. Sales soared.

Impressed with the quality and shipping stability of Hershey's new, chewy milk-based caramels, an English importer placed a large candy order, enabling Hershey to secure a $250,000 loan with which he quickly began expanding his business.

By 1893, in addition to the original Lancaster factory, the now incorporated Lancaster Caramel Co. had plants in Mount joy, Pennsylvania, Chicago and Geneva, Illinois, which together employed more than 1,300 workers. Hershey's persistence had finally paid off. And this would prove to be just the beginning.

"Difficulties show men what they are," he says.

When he failed in New York City, he was able to pay his creditors forty cents on the dollar. As soon as he got on his feet financially he returned to New York City and paid his creditors the remaining sixty percent of his indebtedness.

He says "Maybe they weren't surprised when I handed them the money. They never expected I'd make good my promise to return and wipe the slate clean of my indebtedness. I feel much better since that matter has been taken care of. "

At this time. His Aunt Mattie who had lent him money to open his first business passed away,

"Many a time I've wondered what would have become of me if she hadn't given me a helping hand," he says.

During a visit to the 1893 World's Columbian Exposition in Chicago, Hershey witnessed a demonstration of chocolate-rolling machinery from Germany that sparked a new determination in him. Hershey turned to a friend and said, "Caramels are a fad, but chocolate is permanent. I'm going to make chocolate."

He bought his first chocolate-making equipment from this German company, the J.M. Lehmann Company, in 1893. He was so fascinated by it that he purchased two of the actual pieces of machinery he saw on display at the exposition, and then later bought additional equipment directly from the company's New York office.

He established the Hershey Chocolate Company in 1894 as a subsidiary of the caramel company.

He began producing more than 114 different types of chocolate candies, including the product that would make his name famous the world over, the milk chocolate Hershey Bar. Previously manufactured only in Switzerland and Germany, milk chocolate was new to the United States, and the Hershey Bar became an instant phenomenon.

He knew chocolate was the future. In 1898, He and his sweetheart Catherine who he met in New York decided to marry and they had their marriage in the rectory of St. Patrick's Cathedral in New York.

On August 10, 1900, he sold his caramel company for $1 million, an extraordinarily enormous sum in 1900 and relinquished the Lancaster factory, the caramel recipes, and the "Crystal A" trademark.

"I failed three times because I had not taken the time to get all the facts. After that I learned my lesson well, " he says.

He kept the rights to make chocolate and also use all of his chocolate-making equipment, and rented a wing of the caramel factory to continue his chocolate-making venture.

He turned his attention solely to chocolate. At that time, chocolates were very expensive and were enjoyed only by the rich.

For several years, he had been working at perfecting a viable recipe for making and mass-producing milk chocolate, a process which up to then had been kept a closely guarded secret by the Swiss. Finally, through trial and error, he hit upon the right formula of milk, sugar, and cocoa.

Now with the wealth generated from the sale of the caramel company, he could put that plan into action.

"My experience has shown me that the people who are exceptionally good in business aren't so because of what they know, but because of their insatiable need to know more," says Hershey.

He was always inspired by the utopian "city of the future" created at the Columbian Exposition, So Hershey set out to build not just a chocolate factory, but the ideal town where the workforce could live, play, work and prosper.

Because of its rich supply of clean water, proximity to some of the finest dairy farms in the country, and plenty of land for expansion, Hershey chose his birthplace, Dairy Church, Pennsylvania, as the site for his dream city.

In 1903, Hershey broke ground for his new factory and set into motion the events that would turn his dream into a reality. The factory was modern in every way, with high-tech machinery that eliminated the cost and tedium of making and wrapping chocolate by hand, and made possible the mass production of high-quality milk chocolate at affordable prices.

"You can only make money by giving people what they want," he says.

Construction on the factory began on March 2, 1903, and ended in 1905.

The community Hershey built for his employees was just as impressive and modern. It featured affordable housing with sewage and electricity, paved streets, with names like Chocolate Avenue and Cocoa Avenue, schools, department stores, a trolley system, churches, a library, a hospital, a zoo, an open-air theater, and even an amusement park.

The town was officially renamed to Hershey, Pennsylvania in 1905. Unofficially, It is still called the chocolate town.

Both the community and the company prospered, and by 1915, the chocolate plant alone covered 35 acres.

In 1907, he introduced a new candy. They were bite-sized,

flat-bottomed, conical-shaped pieces of chocolate that he named "Hershey's Kiss". Initially, they were individually wrapped by hand in squares of aluminum foil.

These were an instant hit. In 1921, he eliminated hand wrapping and with the introduction of machine wrapping, he simplified the process and added a small paper ribbon to the top of the package to indicate that it was a genuine Hershey product.

Today, 80 million of the candies are produced each day. Company sales rocketed from $600,000 in 1901 to $20 million by 1921.

"Give them quality. That's the best kind of advertising in the world," he said.

"I didn't follow the policies of those already in the business. If I had, I would never have made a go of it. Instead, I started out with the determination to make a better nickel chocolate bar than any of my competitors made, and I did so." he says.

Hershey continued to introduce new Chocolates. In 1925, they introduced Mr. Goodbar containing peanuts in milk chocolate.

In 1926, they introduced Hershey's Syrup, in 1928, semisweet chocolate chips and in 1938 the Krackel Bar containing crisped rice.

While everything was going well, another disaster stuck Milton.

Kitty. his dear wife had a progressive neurological disease that was never fully diagnosed. She died in 1915 at the age of 42.

They had only been married for 17 years and did not have any children. Even though he could get married again, since he was still young, Milton never remarried and supposedly carried a picture of his late wife wherever he traveled.

Hershey also owned sugar plantations and mills in Cuba from 1916 until 1946.

The operations included 60,000 acres of land, five raw sugar mills, a peanut oil plant, henequen plant, four electric plants, and 251 miles of railroad track with sufficient locomotives and cars.

His flagship sugar mill was located at "Central Hershey" in Cuba. The town that was created to support the mill was developed as a model town and featured many of the same types of services that Hershey had established in "his" town in Pennsylvania.

When the stock market crashed in 1929 and the great depression set in, Hershey refused to let the dark shadow of the Depression fall over his idyllic community. While other companies fired employees and cut back their operations, Hershey embarked on an ambitious building plan devised solely to keep his workers employed.

"One is only happy in proportion as he makes others feel happy," he says.

Profits from his sugar business in Cuba helped sustain the Pennsylvania town during the Great Depression. It was with this money that Milton was able to embark on his "Great Building Campaign".

They constructed a new high school, a sports arena, a community building, and a lavish 170-room hotel.

Legend has it, that during construction of the hotel, Hershey was watching a steam shovel in operation when a foreman proudly commented that it could do the job of 40 workers. Hershey told the foreman to get rid of the shovel and hire 40 workers.

"We should deal with one another not as classes but as persons, as brothers. The more closely we work together, the more effectively we can contribute to the better health of all mankind; this should be our common objective and its achievement would make the world a happier place in which to live," he says.

Both the company and the town survived the Depression and

continued to flourish, thanks to Hershey's singular vision and amazing inventiveness.

He believed that every person had some inherent greatness in them.

He says "Take a man of fair intelligence, give him a fair chance, and he will soon learn to do anything that any other intelligent man is doing."

During World War II, he oversaw the development of the high-energy Field Ration D bars carried by GIs serving in the war zones. The 4-ounce non-melting chocolate bars packed 600 calories and could support soldiers if no other food was available.

Hershey would later say that the four Navy "E for Excellence" awards bestowed on the Field Ration D bars were among the proudest achievements of his life.

Harry Burnett Reese, was an employee of the Hershey Chocolate Company. He decided he could make a living by making his own candy and he opened the H.B. Reese Candy Company in the same town.

in 1923 he began making candy in his basement at night. In 1928, he introduced Peanut butter cups as part of his assortment. In 1942, due to war rationing, Reese eliminated everything except for peanut butter cups from his product line.

Reese got his chocolate from the Hershey Chocolate Company and always enjoyed a good relationship with the company. All of his peanut butter cups bore the banner, "Made in Chocolate Town, So They Must Be Good."

Reese candy also became famous in a short while. By the year 1956, it had yearly sales of around $14 million.

Reese died in 1956 and was succeeded by his six sons. In 1963 they sold the company to Hershey Chocolate Corporation for $23 million.

Today The Hershey Company continues to produce Reese's peanut butter cups, which have become its most popular candy.

Hershey town remains a major tourist attraction to this day.

Each year, nearly 3 million people take the free chocolate-making tour here to learn how chocolate goes from bean to bar.

The facility opened in 1973. Since then, more than 75 million visitors have passed through its doors.

Chocolate World is home to the world's largest selection of Hershey's products found anywhere.

To those who knew Hershey, his generosity wasn't surprising. Shy and reserved, Hershey's quiet demeanor contrasted greatly with many of America's other business titans. While he seldom wrote or read, and had been forced to leave school early, Hershey was driven to make sure those around him received a great education. His display of wealth was rather modest, if not downright thrifty.

His house and the community he'd helped create meant everything to him. When it came to building his own home, he made sure the Hershey Company headquarters was part of the view.

Milton Hershey firmly believed that an individual is morally obligated to share the fruits of success with others. As a result, he made many philanthropic contributions to society, the most prominent of which is the Hershey Industrial School.

Saddened because they had no children of their own, Hershey and his wife, Catherine, established the school in 1909 , so poor, orphaned boys could have a good home and a better chance at life.

To ensure its future, Hershey donated an estimated $60 million to the school in trust, as well as 40 percent of his company's common stock. The school's charter mission was to train young men in useful trades and occupations, but over time its vocational emphasis shifted to college preparation and business curricula, and several of its graduates went on to become executives and officers of the Hershey Foods Corp.

Known today as the Milton Hershey School, the 10,000-acre

institution provides housing and education for nearly 1900 boys and girls whose family life has been disrupted.

In keeping with the work ethic, his mother instilled in him, Hershey continued to work well into his 80s. Hershey remained at the helm of his chocolate empire until 1944, when he finally retired as chairman of the board at the age of 87.

It may seem surprising today when the cost of the average chocolate bar is about 50 cents, but at one time, chocolate was considered a luxury. Before the early 1900s, all chocolate was handmade through a time-consuming and costly process that made chocolate a very expensive treat, affordable only by the rich.

But Milton Hershey was determined to change that. Like Henry Ford, whose assembly line process modernized the automobile industry, Hershey modernized the chocolate industry.

By developing and using innovative machinery that eliminated the need to make and wrap chocolate by hand, Hershey introduced the first method for mass-producing chocolate at affordable prices, allowing everyone to experience the joys of his magical creation, the Hershey Bar.

"If I rest, I'll rust," he says.

He spent the 88th and final year of his life still experimenting with new confections, including celery, carrot and potato ice creams and a surprisingly successful beet sorbet.

In 1945, the world was saddened by the passing away of chocolate legend Milton Hershey and a wonderful human being, who always cared for others.

Shortly after Hershey's death in 1945, the chairman of the board of the National City Bank of New York would proclaim, "Milton Hershey was a man who measured success, not in dollars, but in terms of a good product to pass on to the public, and still more in the usefulness of those dollars for the benefit of his fellow men."

He always remembered his mother's advice which guided him

throughout his life. He says "When I left home as a boy to tackle the job of making a living my mother gave me some good advice. She said, 'Milton, you are now going out into the world to make a man of yourself. My best advice to you is, when you tackle a job stick to it until you have mastered it.' I never have forgotten those words and now when I think of the chocolate business and the way it has grown I think it was my mother's advice that spurred me on and helped me to overcome my obstacles. "

His legacy as a businessman and philanthropist continues to this day. The Hershey Chocolate Company has endured as one of the world's greatest candy makers, with brands that include Almond Joy, Mounds, Cadbury, Reese's and Twizzlers.

"Business is a matter of human service," he says.

Hershey became the largest chocolate manufacturer in the united states. Now Hershey' chocolates are sold in over 60 countries worldwide and Hershey now generates more than $7 billion dollars a year.

He says "My success is the result of not being satisfied with mediocrity, and in making the most of my opportunities. "

"Without faith -- in our work and in ourselves-- we cannot succeed in a long measure in life's undertaking"

He adds "You can surmount failure. You can be battered down three times, as I was, and still come out on top."

11
LIFEISGOOD

SELLING ON THE STREETS TO A $100+ MILLION COMPANY BUILT ON OPTIMISM

Is it possible to invest $200 and make millions from a simple philosophy of "Do what you like, like what you do"
Is it possible to bring happiness to millions of people with just this simple message.

Bert and John were hawking T-shirts on the streets and in college dorms for five years before they hit on the "Life is good" message. Today it is a $100+ million company.

Let us see how Bert and John Jacobs did it.

John and Bert Jacobs grew up as the youngest of six children in the Boston suburb of Needham, Massachusetts. Their mother was a very optimistic person and she instilled this strong character in her kids.

This optimism was especially important for the boys. When they were in elementary school, their parents were in a near-death car accident from which their mother managed to escape with just a few broken bones, but their father lost the use of his right hand.

The stress and frustration from his physical therapy caused him to develop a harsh temper. "He did a lot of yelling when we were in grade school," John says.

"There were often difficult things happening around the house," the brothers say, But their mom, Joan, still believed life was good.

Even when these difficult situations were happening around their house, their mother would still be singing, telling stories, and acting out children's books for them.

"That optimism was something that our family always had, even when we had little else," says John.

After the brothers came out from their college in 1989, they had one question which was, what were they going to do with their lives. They thought hard about it and finally decided to do something with their passion which was art. They decided to do Art on T-shirts.

Both the brothers had always liked to draw when they were kids, so when they finished college they were looking for ways to feature their art. T-shirts seemed to be an accessible way for them to do that. So they started designing shirts and taking them out to try to sell them.

The brothers moved back in, with their parents and started selling a variety of T-shirt designs under the name "Jacob's Gallery". Was it an Instant hit. "Not even close," John says.

For a year, they sold their T-shirts on the streets of Boston. They noticed that they could sell more around college dorms. They decided to hawk their t-shirts in college dorms.

So, they invested $2,100 in an old used van and began their road trips up and down the east coast. The trips lasted about a month or sometime six weeks and after this, they would return back to their home.

Their Van was nicknamed "The Enterprise" because it literally contained their entire enterprise, their T-shirts and them. John says everybody who did not see the van thought, it was a cool van, like a Volkswagen but it really wasn't. It was like a Plymouth Voyager, a soccer mom van.

Even though they were making many trips to the college dorms to sell their T-shirts, they did not have much sales.

"We tried and failed a thousand times," John says about their T-shirt-selling road trips

They tried to figure out, if it was because the designs were bad or if the students had no money, or was it because they were waking them up at 1 a.m. to ask if they wanted to buy a T-shirt.

"When you try, you either succeed or you learn."   "In both, you win," John says.

After hawking their T-shirts at the college dorms, Bret and John would come back to Boston with the idea of creating something new and they would hit the road again.

Most of the nights, they pulled the seats out of the back of the van and would sleep there on top of the T-shirts. During the road trips, since they did not have much money, they tried to live as cheaply as possible.

They made a bit of a game out of keeping expenses very low and would compete with each other, on who would spend less in a day or a week.

John says "If we weren't sleeping in the van, we would find a lounge or dorm to sleep in, but we certainly weren't going to pay for a hotel. We had a journal with an "in" and "out" column, and there was very little in that "out" column other than gas and the occasional bite to eat."

Asked if the students blew them off, when they knocked the dorm doors,

Bert says "A lot of times they would assume we were students, then when they learned what we were doing, rather than being taken aback, they would get a kick out of it. Unlike normal homes where people might be a little more guarded about door-to-door sales, college students welcomed it."

John adds "There's a bit of a romance to the open road and the adventure, especially at that age, so students were intrigued to hear stories from the road trips. During the hours when it didn't make sense to sell in the dorms, like the morning, we would just throw a frisbee in the middle of campus. We just felt so lucky to be traveling, meeting people and creating, even though we were wildly unsuccessful financially."

Both John and Bert lived on peanut butter and jelly sandwiches, most of the time and since they did not have any hotel rooms to stay, they showered only occasionally. "We did drink beer if someone offered it to us," Bert says.

Back in Boston, they would bump into people they knew, and they would ask the brothers, what they were doing. When they told them that they were selling T-shirts, they would tell them that they since they had a college education, they should get a job.

Initially, they ignored this advice. But after some time, when they did not get enough money from selling t-shirts, they thought they should abandon the business and maybe take a job.

But instead of closing down the business, they both took jobs as substitute teachers in an effort to supplement their income.

They continued to go on road trips to sell their T-shirts. They faced several problems.

One time they went on separate road trips. On one of those cold winter nights, John slept in a dorm lounge, but the campus police kicked him out at 3 a.m. It was around zero degrees outside. At this time, John felt, if this was all worth it.

"It was just a pathetic kind of evening, where you question everything," John says.

When in Boston, they were running into friends who had legitimate jobs and wore suits. The brothers were not sure if they should have chosen a job, instead of going out on their own.

"We were getting into our mid- and late-20s, and they seemed to have everything going for them," John says. But the brothers were still living paycheck to paycheck.

At the same time, Bert's girlfriend broke up with him after her mom gave her a quick dose of reality. "He's almost 30 years old, and he still shares a van with his brother. You need to get real," she told her.

But the brothers knew that if they listened to the doubters, they would have to take the safe route, and miss out on realizing their full potential.

They continued to believe in their products and continued their road trips selling their apparels. Sometimes they would have four or five-hour drive between colleges. During one of this driving trip, they got the beginning glimpses of the idea that would turn their life around.

On this trip, they got into a long discussion on how the media tends to focus on the negative things in the world, sometimes the 6 p.m. news only seems to focus on what's wrong.

Bert says " We talked about it for days and eventually came to the conclusion that the media tends to prey on people's fears simply because it sells. So we wondered if there was room to create some symbol of optimism, a hero whose power is the way he views the world."

They talked about how difficult it was to stay positive in such a negative world.

"But what if there was someone who was always happy no matter what was happening?" they wondered. John took that conversation and drew a person, a bohemian guy with a beret and sunglasses and a big smile. They did not name this guy, but later on by accident they had to name him Jake.

He drew the beret on him to show open-mindedness, the smile because he always finds a reason to be happy, and the sunglasses because they wanted to show that it was cool to be optimistic. It was a very simple, childlike drawing.

Every time, they come back to Boston, they had this tradition, where they would throw a keg party. During this keg party, they would put up new ideas on the walls and would let people write comments.

They would host this party, no matter how discouraging the sales were, during their recent trip.

The parties were a win-win because the brothers would provide free beer and entertaining stories from their trips and friends would provide honest feedback on new T-shirt ideas.

After this recent trip, they checked their bank balance and it had just $78. They were not sure if they should throw a party.

But, John and Bert mustered up the courage to throw another party, perhaps their last.

They put up Jake's picture on the wall and everyone started talking about it.

During the party, one person wrote a comment on the wall -- "this guy's got life figured out." next to Jake's picture.

They could never identify who wrote that.

The next morning, Bert and John noticed more comments scrawled around the cartoon face than any other drawing – by a large margin.

So they decided to call him smiley face Jake, the nickname they both had since childhood, and decided to put him on a T-shirt. They added the words "Life is good" because that seemed to sum up Jake's outlook as well as their own.

They printed the image on forty-eight shirts and brought them to a street fair in nearby Cambridge. Expectations were not high. Bert was 29, John was 26, and they'd spent the last five and a half years hawking shirts much like this one.

Though they always felt a strong responsibility to convey positive messages on their shirts, they were also trying to run a business. If Jake didn't sell, he'd be out.

When they were kids, at dinner every night, their mother would start by saying, "Tell me something good that happened today."

"Rather than complaining about the day, commiserating about

struggles or opening up the possibility of a fight, she focused everyone on the positive," says John.

"As simple as mom's words were, they changed the energy in the room," "Before we knew it, we were all riffing on the best, funniest, or most bizarre part of our day," adds John.

John says that this daily exercise prevented them from developing a victim's mentality of "Oh, you wouldn't believe this horrible thing that happened to me today."

Instead of griping about a teacher or homework assignment, he says that they would be laughing about a silly haircut a classmate got that day or a neat project they worked on at school.

Growing up with a mother like theirs, one who sang in the kitchen, told animated stories, and acted out children's books for them, no matter what bad situation they were going through, taught them an important lesson: Being happy isn't dependent on your circumstances.

Bert says "She showed us that optimism is a courageous choice you can make every day, especially in the face of adversity." "It was a great life lesson and business lesson. By starting with what's good, whatever you focus on will grow."

"Some people have an image of Life is good, that we're eating ice cream and throwing a Frisbee around all day and everything comes easy," Bert says. "The reality is we're competitive. The fact we're optimistic doesn't mean we don't have moments or days of doubt and fear, like anybody has."

Bert adds "But optimists are different in how they view those fears, as they choose to focus on the positive over the negative. " Bert says it's what he learned from his mom who is a "tremendous optimist."

"While there were plenty of challenges growing up, my mom focused on what was right in the world and the family," recalls Bert.

Bert says "I remember her driving John and me to the grocery store and realizing she had no money. She turned the car around and smiled. I asked 'Why are you so happy?' She said, 'It's tough I can't get what I need, but on the other hand sometimes I like running out of money because I don't have to decide what's for dinner.' It was ridiculous and we laughed, but it was about seeing the glass half-full."

At the Chicago fair, where they were hawking their newly created t-shirts with Jake and "Life is good" message they were not expecting much sales. To their utter amazement, by noon, all forty-eight shirts were gone. They even sold the ones which they were wearing.

What startled the brothers most was the wide diversity of people who loved the cartoon, punks and preppies, teenagers and grandparents, older married couples and young hipsters. "We'd never seen anything like it," Bert says.

"People 'got it' and they bought it. No explanation was necessary," Bert adds.

The brothers were ecstatic, they had finally found the message they wanted to share and people loved it.

"We were searching for so many years for, 'What do we stand for?'" John says. "Then when we put out this design, the response was so immediate. It was exactly what we had hoped for."

This is when the brothers realized that they had something big on their hands.

"Finally, we had something that had a demand and seemed to have a broad appeal," says John. "We noticed that first day that there were a lot of people buying that shirt, from bikers to teachers. It confirmed that people would be drawn to something that was more positive. It was exciting and scary because we needed to learn how to run a business. We had been traveling around and having a lot of fun. Now we had something that had demand, so we started to figure out the nuts and bolts of the business and how retail worked."

Sensing demand, they decided to sell more but they were disappointed. They loaded up their van with high spirits and went to a lot of shops around Boston, Not one shop wanted to sell their T-shirts. Disappointed, they decided to try one last store. It was a small flip-flop shop on Cape Cod. Nancy, the owner, liked the T-shirts and bought 24 shirts and asked, "What's the smiley guy's name?"

Thinking on the spot, they said, "Jake" because it was short for Jacobs. Later, they discovered that this was a stroke of genius because "Jake" is an old term for "everything's all right."

The shirts sold out in two weeks.

Using what they had learned from their days on the road, they began selling their products to different mom-and-pop stores in Boston and Cape Cod. All these stores helped them evolve their Jake character too.

The first retailer they sold to was a mom-and-pop store -- they asked if Jake likes to eat ice cream. And we said, "He will if you put in an order." Bert says.

John says "We were open. We never considered ourselves brilliant businessmen. But retailers kept calling and asking, "Does Jake fish? Does Jake ride a bike?" That led to an expansion of the product line."

Stores started reordering the product right away.

With demand picking up for the feel-good shirts, the brothers decided to take a leap and hire their first employee, Kerrie Gross, the "adorable 23-year-old" who lived an apartment above the brothers.

When they hired her as "business manager," they asked her what the least amount of money she could earn to pay off her bills was. She said $17,000, and they agreed to that

By the end of the year, the company had done $262,000 in top-line sales and had successfully paid their first employee.

Confident in their sales, the brothers upgraded their office to a 40-foot shipping container on a dirt lot in 1996.

During this time, they sent unique invoices to their customers that included the photo of them in the shipping container and this humorous note: "Please pay on time, so we can keep these lights on and pay our hungry warehouse staff."

In 1997, Life is Good broke $1 million in sales, and they celebrated by hiring three new employees and moving into their first real office in Needham, Massachusetts, where they made it their mission to continue establishing a company culture that welcomed humor at the office.

When asked Why they should be humorous, John says "Because laughter relaxes us, it ambles us to think more clearly as well as communicate and solve problems more effectively,"

Slowly they started expanding and were producing millions of dollars in sales.

John says "We made a million business mistakes between that first day in the streets and where we are today because we just didn't have the business acumen."

One time, they sourced all their production from a single vendor, which is not a good idea as they later found out. The brothers did not do their homework and the vendor didn't deliver on time. All the retailers were waiting for the products.

They frantically worked with the vendor and got the products but it was after a huge delay. That almost put them out of business, but they narrowly escaped.

About Jake and the Life is good message, John says "That brand shows us that, for most of us, happiness is a choice. Some people face difficult adversity, but Jake reminds us to take control of that choice and appreciate what we have instead of thinking of what we could have."

Since year one after starting Life is good, the brothers received letters and emails from people who have been through great adversity, saying "thanks for the hat, that helped me through chemo," or "thanks for the shirt, that embodied how my brother lived, we all wore it to his memorial service."

The more these incredibly moving letters came in, the

brothers realized the depth of their message, especially to people facing difficult times.

One of the most touching stories came from a 11-year-old girl named Lindsey Beggan who had terminal bone cancer. She was always wearing Life is good apparel when she was being interviewed by the media.

She had about a year to live, and they would ask her, why she was wearing a shirt that says Life is good, and she said, "Before I was sick, I took my life for granted, but now that I might not live as long, I want to make sure I enjoy and appreciate it every day."

Bert says "She was really the first one to zero in on the depth of the message. After that, we heard hundreds of other stories like that." Even more inspiring was that Lindsey Beggan survived, graduated from college and today remains cancer-free."

Life is good continued to grow and moved past $3 million in sales. Both John and Bert continued to live simple lifestyles.

"For some people, making a lot of money can be really challenging, because there's an appetite for a bunch of boats or houses. We always joke that after we got new mountain bikes, we didn't know what to do." Bert says.

John adds "We were lucky to grow up in a house which was chaotic and small, with six kids in all, but thanks to our parents, we got a sense of what is really fulfilling -- as corny as it sounds, it's friends, family, laughter, and love. Everything else is secondary. So getting to share this message with more people is the funnest thing in the world."

Life is good continued to grow and many suitors wanted to buy it, but Jake and Brett were not interested.

When everything seemed to be going well, an unfortunate event happened that threatened the company's future and questioned their core message.

On 9/11 the Twin towers attack happened. Even their employees began to question the company's entire outlook; maybe life in America wasn't so good, at least not right then.

But a woman in the firm's shipping department suggested holding fundraisers for families who had lost loved ones in the attack. So they created an American flag T-shirt emblazoned with the words "Life is good" and raised $207,000 in just two months, a significant sum for a company with only $3 million in sales at the time.

Thus began the company's commitment to charitable causes, which has generated $6.5 million over the last decade. In 2006, the company established its own foundation to help kids overcome life-threatening challenges such as violence, illness, and extreme poverty.

When Haiti was devastated by an earthquake in 2010, the company made a long-term commitment to raise money for victims using images like Jake holding a Haitian flag, and later created a play-based program for the country's affected children. "Optimism has no borders," Bert says.

The company's fundraising events reflect its quirky culture. The Life is good Pumpkin Festival was held on Boston Common in 2006 broke the Guinness World Record for the most carved, lit pumpkins in one place at one time. All proceeds went to the Life is good Kids Foundation.

Their social mission was to help kids overcome life-challenging situations, which is a subcategory of the company's mission to spread optimism. says Bert, whose official title is Chief Executive Optimist. "With play therapy for kids facing violence, you're teaching them the importance of engaging in the world and seeing the glass half-full. "

Life is good continued to grow and hired 160 employees and is now generating around $100million. The brothers did all this without advertising and it was mostly word of mouth.

Life is good started expanding into other categories too. They now sell a variety of apparel, pet products, a stationery line and footballs, frisbees and other recreational products in about 30 countries and 5,000 retailers in the United States, including 100 dedicated Life is good stores.

"Children have always been the greatest inspiration for us," Bert says. "Being open-minded is a key component to optimism. The most open-minded people are children; their lives are wide open."

"We'd like to become a hub of optimism, a place where people can go, in both digital and physical space, to share stories about the power of optimism," says Bert.

"To be able to turn the fun things you do in your life into your work and have a positive impact on the world around you is a dream to us," Bert adds.

Bert stresses the importance of believing in what you do, regardless of what it is. "Don't get involved with something simply because it could work. Get involved in something combined with the love of your life. Then I think you greatly increase your chance of success. You're pouring the things that are most meaningful to you into your work. Eventually, your customers read that."

They got lots of offers to sell the business or go public, but they wanted to see how far they can take this. "We've come a long way but at the same time we feel very much like we're just getting started," Bert says.

Both John and Bert are in demand as motivational speakers. They donate all their speaking fees.

They also wrote a book called Life is Good: How to live with Purpose and enjoy the ride.

Bert says."Business is just a tool for you to accomplish whatever you want to accomplish in your life. I don't care about the clothing business. That's just a vehicle for a message."

"We're just trying to do something special with our lives. That's the way people have to choose their careers, really think about what you want to do with your life and then find something to use to do that. "

"When you're old and gray and you've spent your one precious life, what will you have spent it on? What would make you happy?"

Brothers John and Bert wanted to do something with their passion, which was art.

They started a T-shirt business, but they had dismal sales. They took up part-time teaching jobs to survive. Their friends were successful in their jobs and these two were failures with not much money coming from their T-shirt business. They were close to giving up, but their mother's inspiration kept them forward. When they were young and their life was chaotic and stressful, their mother used to be optimistic and used to see the good things from the bad things which were happening to them and remained joyful.

The brothers remained optimistic and they created Life is good Apparels based on Optimism.

To save money, they ate peanut butter sandwiches, slept in their van and faced many harsh difficulties. But slowly, customers loved their products and it grew beyond their wildest dreams and exceeded $100+ million in revenue.

The brothers attribute all of their company's success to the contagiousness of their mission, "To spread the power of optimism," which they learned from their mother early on.

"We want to spread this message and help people understand the depth of what that means," John says. "It's not that life is easy or life is perfect. It's that life is good."

12

WHATSAPP

A POOR BOY LIVING ON FOOD STAMPS TO A MULTI-BILLIONAIRE

Jan Koum migrated to America in his teens. He was poor and did not know proper English.

He endured many personal losses and setbacks, yet he built WhatsApp, one of the most widely used app in the whole wide world.

His life reveals an incredible rise-and-fall of winning, losing, and winning again. If you didn't believe in the power of persistence before, read on to uncover this amazing story of this remarkable geek.

If you ever experienced failure and sulked in self-defeat, this real-life entrepreneur story will remove the shackles of self-defeat from your mind and will inspire you to keep moving forward.

Sit back, relax, grab a popcorn. Let us check out this awe-inspiring rags-to-riches story.

Jan Koum was born on February 24, 1976, to Jewish parents and raised in a small village outside of Kiev, Ukraine. He was the only child of a housewife and a construction manager who built hospitals and schools. His house had no hot water, and his parents rarely talked on the phone in case it was tapped by the state.

He lived a simple life in a small town that was disrupted by the chaotic political environment and anti-Semitism in the country.

Life for the Koum family was far from luxurious, with simple surroundings, basic living conditions coupled with a constant and ongoing fear of the secret police who had extensive invasive powers and were never reluctant to use them, especially among members of the Jewish community.

Jan says "I grew up in a country where I remember my parents not being able to have a conversation on the phone. The walls had ears, and you couldn't speak freely."

His school was in a bad shape. It was so run-down, that it didn't even have an inside bathroom.

"Imagine the Ukrainian winter, -20°C, where little kids have to stroll across the parking lot to use the bathroom. Society was extremely closed off" Jan says.

He adds "There were a lot of negatives, of course, but there were positives to living a life unfettered by possessions. It gave us the chance to focus on education, which was very important."

It was for that reason, in 1992 when the gates to Jewish immigration from the former Soviet Union opened, that his family decided that life would be better for them in the United States. Jan was just 16 when he, his mother and his grandmother left the little village outside of Kiev to start a new life, with his father remaining behind with plans to join them later.

By some quirk of fate, they arrived in the town of Mountain View, situated in Santa Clara County, in the San Francisco Bay

Area of California. At that time Mountain View was a pleasant little town which offered low-cost affordable housing, where they found themselves a compact two-bedroom apartment which they could afford to rent with the help of government assistance.

Things were tough for Jan Koum growing up in a new country, especially when he had to come together with the reality that his father may not be coming to live with his family in America.

Jan's mother had stuffed their suitcases with pens and a stack of 20 Soviet-issued notebooks to avoid paying for school supplies in the U.S. She took up babysitting and Jan swept the floor of a grocery store to help make ends meet.

Then another disaster struck this young kid. Not long after they arrived in the United States, his mother was diagnosed with cancer.

This new situation meant that she was unable to work to support her son and her ailing mother, and his family was forced to live off disability allowance.

Many days, Jan would wait patiently in line to collect the food stamps that they needed to get their food. The food stamps were issued by the united states government for low-income families.

These were difficult and testing times and Jan would recall his anger and frustration of being unable to contact his father and the rest of his family and friends that he had left behind in Ukraine.

The secret police in Ukraine could spy on the phone conversations and no one could speak freely.

The only way for Jan to contact them was through the telephone which was both expensive from the united states and not secure, and he was hoping that one day there would be a way for people from across the world to keep in touch with each other cheaply and securely.

Jan's father who remained in Ukraine became ill and eventually passed away in 1997 and could not make it to the United

States. Jan was heart-broken and sad and he had no way to go back to Ukraine and see his father before he was buried.

Jan joined the local school. He was the only kid in class whose family didn't have a car, so he had to get up at 6 am to get the bus and get to school. He slowly learned English and began to speak good English. "Growing up in Ukraine is not easy, and prepares you for a lot of things physically and mentally." he says.

At school, he disliked the casual, flighty nature of American high-school friendships. He says "in Ukraine, you went through ten years with the same, small group of friends at school. you really learn about a person."

Jan was a troublemaker at school but by age 18, he had also taught himself computer programming by purchasing manuals from a used bookstore.

He joined a hacker group called w00w00 on the Efnet internet relay chat network and did a few bold things like hacking into the servers of Silicon Graphics and chatted with Napster co-founder Sean Fanning who was in the same hacker group too.

He enrolled at San Jose State University and to pay for college he moonlighted at Ernst & Young as a security tester.

In 1997, he found himself assigned to the then-fledgling search engine Yahoo, to inspect security levels at the company's advertising system, working in conjunction with Brian Acton, Yahoo employee number 44.

Brian Acton the Yahoo employee, recalls his first impressions of Jan being that he was quite a bit different from the other Ernst & Young employees.

He was very no-nonsense, like 'What are your policies here; What are you doing here?'"

Other Ernst & Young people were using "touchy-feely" tactics like gifting bottles of wine, but Jan was "Whatever, Let's cut to the chase."

It turned out Jan liked Brian's no-nonsense style too. "Neither of us has an ability to bullshit," says Jan.

Brian Acton grew up in suburban Florida playing golf, his adoptive father had attempted a professional golf career, while his mother had built an air-freight business.

Six months later, Jan interviewed at Yahoo and got a job as an infrastructure engineer. Brian was the one who was interviewing Jan.

Jan was still studying at San Jose State University when he joined Yahoo. About two weeks into his job at Yahoo, one of the company's servers broke. Yahoo co-founder David Filo called Jan's mobile for help. "I'm in class," Jan answered discreetly. "What the f*** are you doing in class?" David Filo shrilled. "Get your ass into the office."

Filo had a small team of server engineers and needed all the help he could get. "I hated school anyway," Jan says. So, later on, he dropped out of college.

In 2000, his mother got really sick and she passed away. Jan was suddenly alone and felt extremely sad.

At this time in his life when he felt alone and depressed, Brian, the Yahoo employee and now his friend reached out to him and supported him. He would invite Jan to his house. Slowly the two started to go out skiing together and played soccer and ultimate Frisbee.

Over the next nine years, the pair also watched Yahoo go through multiple ups and downs. Brian got some money from his Yahoo stock and invested in companies in the dotcom boom, but lost all his money in the ensuing 2001 stock market bust.

Jan and Brian remained as colleagues at Yahoo for nine years, during which time a firm friendship developed between them.

During this time, Brian helped launch Yahoo's advertising platform, Project Panama in 2006.

Brian slowly lost interest in his job. He says "Dealing with ads is depressing, You don't make anyone's life better by making advertisements work better." He was emotionally drained.

"I could see it on him in the hallways," says Jan, who wasn't enjoying things either. In his LinkedIn profile, Jan unenthusiastically describes his last three years at Yahoo with the words, "Did some work."

On October 31, 2007, Jan and Brian finally quit Yahoo and took a year to decompress, traveling around South America and playing ultimate Frisbee.

After they came back, both of them applied for jobs at Facebook and failed in the interview. "We're part of the Facebook reject club," Brian says.

Meanwhile, Jan was eating into his $400,000 savings from Yahoo and drifting, not knowing what to do next.

Then in January 2009, Jan bought an iPhone and realized that the seven-month-old App Store was about to spawn a whole new industry of apps.

During this time, he became frustrated with his local gym's ban on using mobile phones, because he kept missing calls as he was working out. He had been trying to come up with an iPhone app, and his initial idea was to allow people to set statuses on their phones, so that their contacts could see what they were up to at any given moment, for instance, "Can't talk, at the gym."

During this time, he used to visit the home of Alex Fishman, a Russian friend who would invite the local Russian community to his place in West San Jose for weekly pizza and movie nights. Up to 40 people sometimes showed up.

Both Jan and Alex Fishman became friends and Jan told Alex about his app idea. Jan also showed Alex, his Russian friend his address book and explained his idea.

Whenever they met, they stood for hours talking about Jan's idea for the app over tea at Alex Fishman's kitchen counter.

Alex says "His thinking was it would be really cool to have statuses next to individual names of the people." The statuses would show if you were on a call, your battery was low, or you were at the gym.

Jan could do the backend, but he needed an iPhone developer, so Alex introduced Jan to Igor Solomennikov, a developer in Russia that he'd found on Rentacoder.com

Jan almost immediately chose the name WhatsApp because it sounded like "what's up" and a week later on his birthday, Feb. 24, 2009, he incorporated WhatsApp Inc. in California. "He's very thorough," says Alex.

The app hadn't even been written yet, but Jan spent days creating the backend code to synch his app with any phone number in the world, pouring over a Wikipedia entry that listed international dialing prefixes. He would spend many infuriating months updating his software for the hundreds of regional nuances.

The early versions of WhatsApp kept crashing or getting stuck and when Alex installed it on his phone, he found that only a handful of the hundreds of numbers on his address book, mostly local Russian friends had downloaded it.

One day while eating out at Tony Roma's in San Jose, Alex went over the problems in WhatsApp and Jan took notes in one of the Soviet-era notebooks his mother had brought over years before and saved for important projects.

Jan became very disheartened because with all his grueling efforts, not many people downloaded and it was still not working properly.

The following month after a game of ultimate Frisbee with Brian, Jan grudgingly admitted he should probably fold up and start looking for a job. Brian balked. "You'd be an idiot to quit now," he said. "Give it a few more months."

The first release, in May 2009, went nowhere. But a month later, Apple introduced push notifications in iOS 3.0, letting developers to push notifications when the users weren't using an app on their phone. This was a game-changer.

Jan updated WhatsApp so that each time you changed your status to "Can't talk, I'm at the gym", it would ping everyone in your network using push notifications. Alex's Russian friends started using it to ping each other with custom statuses like, "I woke up late," or "I'm on my way."

"At some point, it sort of became instant messaging," says Alex. "We started using it as 'Hey how are you?' And then someone would reply."

Jan watched the changing statuses on a Mac Mini at his townhouse in Santa Clara and realized he'd inadvertently created a messaging service. "Being able to reach somebody halfway across the world instantly, on a device that is always with you, was powerful," says Jan.

That led Jan to rethink WhatsApp as a full, cross-platform messenger app that would use the phone's contacts folder as "a prebuilt social network", and the phone number in place of a login.

He had gone through three Skype accounts the previous summer because he couldn't remember his passwords and usernames, and he was determined to make his app "just work".

The only other free texting service around at the time was BlackBerry's BBM, but that only worked among Blackberries. There was Google's G-Talk and Skype, but WhatsApp was unique in that the login was your own phone number.

Jan released WhatsApp 2.0 with a messaging component and watched his active users suddenly swell to 250,000.

He went to see Brian, who was still unemployed and dabbling in another startup idea that wasn't going anywhere.

The two sat at Brian's kitchen table and started sending messages to each other on WhatsApp, At this time, WhatsApp already had the famous double check mark that showed the sender that another phone had received a message and saw it.

Brian realized he was looking at a potentially richer SMS experience. It was also more effective than the so-called MMS messages, which was used for sending photos and other media and he knew that these MMS services often didn't work.

Jan convinced Brian to become a co-founder and Brian agreed.

Brian and Jan worked out of the Red Rock Cafe, a watering hole for startup founders on the corner of California and Bryant in Mountain View. The entire second floor was always full of people with laptops perched on wobbly tables, silently writing code. The two were often up there, Brian scribbling notes and Jan typing.

In October of that year, Brian got five ex-Yahoo friends to invest $250,000 in seed funding.

They started experimenting with business models that would bring in revenue but also ensured controlled growth that their infrastructure could support.

The pair were getting flooded with emails from iPhone users, excited by the prospect of international free texting and were requesting a version for Nokia's and Blackberries because they wanted to "WhatsApp" their friends who were using Nokia's and Blackberries.

Jan hired an old friend who lived in LA, Chris Peiffer to make the BlackBerry version of WhatsApp

Chris was skeptical because he thought people already had SMS and they would not need Whatsapp.

Jan explained that people's texts were actually metered in different countries and Phone companies would charge money if they exceed their texting limits. "It stinks," he told him. "It's a dead technology like a fax machine left over from the seventies, sitting there as a cash cow for carriers." Chris Peiffer looked at the eye-popping user growth and joined.

Jan says "We've taken SMS technology for consumers and improved it."

Next, they needed a cheap office. They found a startup subleasing some cubicles on a converted warehouse on Evelyn

Ave, Sunnyvale. The whole other half of the building was occupied by Evernote. To conserve electricity bill, they wore blankets for warmth and worked off cheap Ikea tables. Even then there was no WhatsApp sign for the office.

When someone wanted directions for attending an interview. They asked them to "Find the Evernote building. Go round the back. Find an unmarked door. Knock".

Both Jan and Brian worked without taking any salaries for the first few early years, but their biggest early cost was sending verification texts to users. Jan and Brian were using SMS brokers like Click-A-Tell, who would send an SMS to the U.S. for 2 cents, but to the Middle East for 65 cents. These costs were draining their money.

Fortunately, WhatsApp was gradually bringing in revenue, roughly about $5,000 a month by early 2010 and enough to cover the costs.

Jan says "Communication is at the very core of our society. That's what makes us human."

They occasionally switched the app from "free" to "paid" so they wouldn't grow too fast.

"We'd grow super fast when we were free, 10,000 downloads a day," recalls Brian. "And when we'd kick over to paid, we'd start declining, down to 1,000 a day."

In Dec. 2009 they updated WhatsApp for the iPhone to send photos and were shocked to see user growth increasing even when it had the $1 price tag.

At this time, they decided to keep charging and not switch back to free. "You know, I think we can actually stay paid," Brian told Jan.

By early 2011 WhatsApp was squarely in the top 20 of all apps in the U.S. Apple App Store. During a dim sum lunch with staff, someone asked Jan why he wasn't calling the press and telling about it. "Marketing and press kick up dust," Jan replied. "It gets in your eye, and then you're not focusing on the product."

Both founders shared a passion for hating advertisement and Jan even has a note on his desk saying "No Ads! No Games! No Gimmicks".

From the start, they refused to carry advertising. Jan refers to his favorite line from Tyler Durden from the movie Fight Club - He says "Advertising has us chasing cars and clothes, working jobs we hate so we can buy shit we don't need."

Jan adds "There's nothing more personal to you than communicating with friends and family, and interrupting that, with advertising is not the right solution," he says "And we don't have to know a lot about our users. To target advertisements well, companies need to know where you are, what you might be doing, who you might be with, what you might like or not like. That's an insane amount of data.

"I grew up in a society where everything you did was eavesdropped on, recorded, snitched on," he says. "I had friends when we were kids getting into trouble for telling anecdotes about Communist leaders."

"Nobody should have the right to eavesdrop, or you become a totalitarian state, the kind of state I escaped as a kid to come to this country where you have democracy and freedom of speech. Our goal is to protect it. We have encryption between our client and our server. We don't save any messages on our servers, we don't store your chat history. They're all on your phone."

He adds "Utilities get out of the way. Can you imagine if you flipped a light switch and had to watch an ad before you got electricity? Can you imagine if you turned on a faucet and had to watch an ad before the water came out?"

Brian and Jan had spent a combined 20 years at Yahoo!, working hard to keep the site working. And yes, working hard to sell ads, because that's what Yahoo! did.

It gathered data and it served pages and it sold ads. Jan says "we watched Yahoo! get eclipsed in size and reach by Google, a more efficient and more profitable ad seller. They knew what you were searching for, so they could gather your data more efficiently and sell better ads.

These days companies know literally everything about you, your friends, your interests, and they use it all to sell ads."

"When we sat down to start our own thing together, we wanted to make something that wasn't just another ad clearinghouse. We knew that we could charge people directly if we could do all those things. We knew we could do what most people aim to do every day, avoid ads."

They also knew that if they focused on ads, most of their engineers time would be spent on optimizing data mining, writing better code to collect all your personal data, upgrading the servers that hold all the data and making sure it's all being logged and collated and sliced and packaged and shipped out.

Instead, they wanted their engineers to focus on the product and make it world-class.

Jan says revenue was not his prime concern. He says "We take a similar approach to Google in search. Remember the portals that came before. Google wants people to leave their site as soon as possible because they'd done a good job. We want you to talk without being interrupted by ads. Monetization is important to us, but we're not sitting here with a bunch of consultants figuring out how to squeeze the last penny out of our users."

In Silicon Valley, industry analysts were at once amazed by WhatsApp's success and skeptical that Brian and Jan could sustain it without having advertisements.

They never advertised WhatsApp nor did any other marketing. It just spread from user to user virally. "We're more interested in building stuff than talking about it," says Jan.

As it grew, Venture capitalists wanted to invest in WhatsApp, but Jan and Brian were against getting any money. Brian saw VC funding as a bailout.

But Sequoia partner Jim Goetz was persistent, spending eight months working his contacts to get either of the founders to agree to meet him. He'd met with a dozen other companies in the messaging space like Pinger, Tango, and Baluga, but it was clear WhatsApp was the leader. To Sequoia Jim's surprise, this startup WhatsApp was already paying corporate income taxes. He had never seen a startup do this in his entire venture investing career.

He eventually got a meeting and he met Jan and Brian at the Red Rock Café. He answered lots and lots of questions to Jan and Brian and promised them that he will not push advertising models on them but act as a strategic advisor.

Jan and Brian eventually agreed to take $8 million investment from Sequoia Capital.

Two years later in Feb. 2013, when WhatsApp's user base had swelled to about 200 million active users and its staff to 50, Brian and Jan agreed it was time to raise some more money.

Brian says the money was for insurance, as a backup in dire situations, if the money runs out for some unknown reason.

Brian recalls his mother, who ran her own freight forwarding businesses, used to lose sleep over making payroll. "You never want to be in a position where you can't make payroll," he says.

They decided to hold a second funding round, in secret. Sequoia would invest another $50 million, valuing WhatsApp at $1.5 billion. At that time Brian took a screenshot of WhatsApp's bank balance and sent it to Sequoia capital's Goetz. It read $8.25 million, still, in excess of all the money, they'd received in their first round of funding from Sequoia two years before.

Even though WhatsApp was growing fast, WhatsApp's office still never had a sign. "I can't see a reason for there being a sign. It's an ego boost," Jan scoffs. "We all know where we work."

They wanted the app to be known for its reliability and simplicity. What kept them awake was the occasional server outage. One time there was a server outage and people were having panic attacks on Twitter. They fixed it quickly.

A whiteboard in the office shows the number of days since

the last outage or incident, as a factory might show a tally for injuries or deaths.

"A single message is like your firstborn child," says Brian, a new parent himself. "We can never drop a message."

A whiteboard lists its 99.92456 percent uptime, with thousands of servers ensuring smooth delivery of millions of messages per second and more than a billion images a day. "Our mission is clear: get out of the way," says Jan.

"The f-word here is focus," Jan adds.

WhatsApp's success boils down to a couple of technical advantages: Jan made it one of the first mobile apps to sync with a phone's contacts.

After he got fed up with forgetting his Skype username and password, he went through the painstaking process of phone-number normalization for WhatsApp, ditching logins and passwords to make his service as simple as sending an SMS. The numbers on your phone are "your real-life network," he says.

Jan and Brian also picked up years of experience at Yahoo in building networks to scale, servers that could handle hundreds of millions of people's data without buckling.

Unlike other startups, which would have ramped up users, Jan and Brian knew to restrain their user growth in the early days.

"Instead of the standard mentality of 'get big fast...'" says Brian. "We took a different approach," Jan adds.

Brian says "We're the most atypical Silicon Valley company you'll come across. We were founded by thirtysomethings; we focused on business sustainability and revenue rather than getting big fast, we've been incognito almost all the time, we're mobile first, and we're global first."

Instead of Amazon cloud services, WhatsApp used dedicated servers that run on sturdy operating systems like FreeBSD, an older alternative to the more-popular Linux and for programming, they used Erlang, a programming language built for telecommunication apps. These decisions gave them a tighter control on infrastructure.

Their no-nonsense commitment to keeping WhatsApp free of advertising and respecting users' privacy is what drew millions of users to the app.

Jan says "Our task is bringing rich, affordable, reliable messaging to every phone in the world. That's our product and that's our passion"

He adds "We won't stop until every single person on the planet has an affordable and reliable way to communicate with their friends and loved ones."

In the spring of 2012, Jan got an email with the subject "Get together?" from Mark Zuckerberg, Facebook founder and Mark requested for a meeting.

WhatsApp was emerging as a global phenomenon. Some 90 million people were using it to text and send photos for free. No social utility had ever grown as fast. Facebook had only 60 million users by its third birthday, and at the time close to half of WhatsApp users were returning daily.

Mark Zuckerberg, Facebook's founder, had been using WhatsApp and wanted to meet Jan over for dinner. Jan stalled, then finally wrote back saying he was traveling soon and dealing with server issues. Zuckerberg suggested they meet before Jan left. Jan forwarded the reply to his co-founder, Brian Acton, and his sole venture backer, Jim Goetz, the partner at Sequoia Capital, adding the word: "Persistent!"

"When someone of Mark's status contacts you directly, you answer the phone," Brian told Jan. He suggested Jan to meet Zuckerberg.

Jan had lunch with Zuckerberg later that month at Esther's German Bakery, chosen for its discreet back patio and located 20 miles away from Facebook's campus. Over their meal, Zuckerberg said he admired what Jan had built and hinted at his interest in combining their two firms.

Slowly Zuckerberg and Jan became friends, meeting once a month or so for dinner.

For the next year, WhatsApp focused on its user growth and it marched past 300 million users. In June 2013 Jan and Brian happened to meet Sundar Pichai, who was overseeing Android and Chrome at Google at that time.

They talked about their love of clean and simple digital products. At some point around early 2014, Pichai decided it would be good for Jan and Brian to meet his CEO at that time, Larry Page. Jan and Brian agreed to meet Larry Page on Tuesday, Feb. 11, 2014.

On the Friday before that meeting, a WhatsApp staffer ran into Facebook's head of business development, Amin Zoufonoun, and told him in a casual talk, that Jan was meeting with Google's Larry Page.

Amin Zoufonoun who helped Facebook's $1 billion Instagram acquisition in April 2012, went back to his company and set the wheels in motion to accelerate an acquisition offer that had already been in the works for some time.

Zuckerberg invited Jan over to his house on Monday night and finally floated the idea of an acquisition that would leave WhatsApp independent and crucially, make Jan a board member of Facebook.

"It was a partnership, where I would help him make decisions about the company," Jan recalls. "The combination of everything that was discussed is what made it very interesting for us."

The next day Jan and Brian drove to Google's Mountain View headquarters and met with Page and Pichai in one of the company's gleaming conference rooms. They talked for an hour about the world of mobile and WhatsApp's goals. "It was a pleasant conversation," says Jan. Page, he adds, is "a smart guy."

When asked if he got the impression that Larry Page was interested in buying WhatsApp, Jan pauses. "No," he says. Maybe there was a hint? "Maybe I'm not good at reading him."

If Larry page was interested, it might have been too late.

Whatsapp continued to grow in other countries too. India had more than 40 million active users. Mexico had over 30 million users, and the UK 17 million.

On Thursday, Jan and Brian went to Zuckerberg's house for dinner at 7 pm., where Brian met Zuckerberg for the first time.

"One day I want you to become bigger than us in the number of users," Zuckerberg told them.

Zuckerberg said he wanted them to keep doing what they were doing but with the might of Facebook's legal, financial and engineering resources.

At 9 pm. Brian went home to tend to his young family. Jan and Zuckerberg played a high-stakes game: One source says that Zuckerberg offered a range of $15 billion and higher and that Jan said he was looking for something closer to $20 billion. Facebook's founder Zuckerberg asked for some time.

On Friday, Feb. 14, 2014, on Valentine's day, Jan got in his car and stopped at Zuckerberg's house for another meeting.

He did not interrupt the Zuckerberg's Valentine's Day meal. "It wasn't like there was dinner and candlelight and I barged in through the door," he says.

Over snacks, Jan and Zuckerberg hammered out the final details of the partnership and WhatsApp's all-important independence under Facebook, but the two weren't yet in agreement.

Finally, on Saturday night Jan and Zuckerberg met again and went from talking in the kitchen to the living room couch before Zuckerberg offered $19 billion as well as deal terms that Jan liked. It was "something we can probably do on our end," Jan replied about the offer.

Jan waited for Zuckerberg to leave the room and got on the phone to Brian, who was at home. It was around 9 p.m. He gave his friend all the finalized details. "Do you want to move forward?" he asked.

"I like Mark," Brian replied. "We can work together. Let's make this deal."

Jan walked out of the room and found Zuckerberg. "I just talked to Brian," Jan said. "He thinks we should work together and that you're a good guy and we should do it."

The two of them shook hands and then hugged. Zuckerberg remarked it was "f***king exciting," and whipped out a bottle of Johnnie Walker Blue Label, which he knew was Jan's favorite Scotch.

They each called their business-development directors to come over and finalize the process. About an hour later Jan drove home in his car and went to bed.

Jan says "A lot of times, people start out with a lot of good ideas, but then they don't execute. They lose the purity of their vision. You end up running around in circles."

On Feb 19th, 2014, WhatsApp was acquired by Facebook for $19 billion. The tech world shook at the insane price.

When the deal happened, WhatsApp had only 56 employees and roughly $20 million in revenue. Facebook later made the app free for all users.

Rather than signing the papers at WhatsApp's headquarters, they drove two blocks, at Sequoia's Jim Goetz's suggestion, to 101 Moffett Boulevard, the abandoned former social services building where Jan once stood in line and collected food stamps as a teenager. Jan signed the papers on the main door.

Jan says "A lot of what I experienced growing up in the U.S.S.R. and coming to the U.S. as an immigrant actually reflects itself in WhatsApp. Experiences from our youth shape what we do later in life."

He adds "We know people go to sleep excited about who they chatted with that day. We want WhatsApp to be the product that keeps you awake… and that you reach for in the morning."

Roughly one in seven people on earth now use WhatsApp and

have the ability to call and text their friends and family for free. More than a Trillion messages pass through WhatsApp.

Living in dire situation in Ukraine, Jan immigrated from to America and faced many personal tragedies like losing his father and not being able to see him and losing his mother to illness.

In his childhood in Ukraine, he and his family were afraid to talk on the phone as it was taped by the government. He had this vision of building an app to let users communicate cheaply and securely throughout the world. And this became the genesis for building WhatsApp.

From a poor boy who couldn't speak proper English to building an app used by more than 1.2 billion people worldwide and selling it for a jaw-dropping $19 billion, Jan Koum had come a long way. He proved that with a penetrating vision and passion, anyone can succeed.

Jan says "We wanted to spend our time building a service people wanted to use because it worked and saved them money and made their lives better in a small way."

"Do one thing, and do it well," Jan adds.

CLOSING WISDOM

"If you can dream it, you can do it."

~Walt Disney, Founder of Disney

BONUS MATERIAL

Can you be a Rich and Successful entrepreneur?
　Find out more at :
　http://www.ideasU.com/1million

ABOUT THE AUTHOR

Vijay Peduru is a popular podcaster, author and the founder of ideasU.com and ideasMagic.com.

His Podcast "How They Made Their Millions" has been ranked in Apple Podcasts top 100 in Business/Careers section.

He is on a quest to find an answer to a simple question: How to be a super-successful entrepreneur?

After reading tons of books , spending boatloads of money (greater than $50,000) on courses, he was still not able to figure this out.

Lucky for him, he studied how the human mind works by deeply studying both the ancient Eastern philosophies and the cutting edge Western scientific studies.

This unique ability allowed him to study humans very keenly and almost accurately.

So, he decided on a simple strategy. To peer into the minds of the world's greatest entrepreneurs and figure out what makes them super-successful.

What he found blew him away. It was almost opposite to what everyone was teaching or writing about in popular books and mainstream lectures.

He shares these inspiring entrepreneur stories and what makes these entrepreneurs successful at ideasU.com.

Vijay lives in San Ramon, a hilly little town close to San Francisco. He loves to do Classical yoga and meditation, the one taught by ancient saints and prefers fresh vegetarian food, except when he goes to parties, he binges on whatever vegetarian food he gets.

Oh, yah,. He is ever-fascinated by the guts and boldness of great entrepreneurs.

If you happen to meet him, he would love if you give him a bunch of baby carrots than a chocolate. Yes, he admits, he was a cute little rabbit in his prior life.

He is on a crusade to inspire aspiring entrepreneurs to go bootstrap the startups they dreamt of starting and to make them Rich, joyful and super-successful.

His goal: To help aspiring entrepreneurs become super-successful, millionaire entrepreneurs..

His message to Entrepreneurs: Keep Rocking and Keep Zooming!.

You can follow him at
   Instagram:
https://www.instagram.com/think.like.a.billionaire/
   Twitter: https://twitter.com/ideasudotcom

www.ingramcontent.com/pod-product-compliance
Lightning Source LLC
LaVergne TN
LVHW051115080426
835510LV00018B/2054